MOMMO'S STORY

Estelle Friedland

outskirts
press

Outskirts Press, Inc.
http://www.outskirtspress.com

Paperback ISBN: 978-1-4787-8543-9
Hardback ISBN: 978-1-4787-8921-5

Outskirts Press and the "OP" logo are trademarks belonging to Outskirts Press, Inc.

PRINTED IN THE UNITED STATES OF AMERICA

There is a song by the title "The Story of My Life" (by Neil Diamond). My son, Flip and my daughter, Lisa, have been bugging me to write some of my stories. I have lots of time and no excuse to keep me from getting started. I am not much of a writer and really do not know where to start. Lisa and Randy bought me a desk and a new laptop computer and keyboard. Lisa's son, Jason, said I had so many stories I had to write them down.

Table of Contents

I'LL BEGIN BY writing about my parents and how they met. My father, Harry, whom I called pop, lived in Maine. His parents were deceased and I never knew them. He had a beautiful sister, Mary, who he adored and two brothers, Sam and David. His oldest sister, Stella, had passed away at an early age. I was named after her.

Pop had a small men's clothing store in Maine in 1914 and went to Boston by bus to buy the merchandise for his store. He needed to replenish his supply of overalls, which the Maine farmers all purchased. The overall factory owner was a very nice distinguished older gentleman and had everything in stock that pop needed. After he took pop's order it was getting late. Instead of going back to Maine by bus that same night, he suggested he stay in Boston overnight. He invited pop to go home with him to his house in the blue hill section of Boston (which was Dorchester) by trolley. He suggested he should have dinner with his family and take the bus back to Maine the following day. He had a very large beautiful home which he needed for his very large family. There were four children from his first marriage. There was one son and three daughters. My mother was one of them. His first wife (my grandmother) passed away at a young age and he was a widower. He remarried a widow who had two daughters so there were already six children. Then they had two sets of twins, two girls and two boys. Altogether there were ten kids--three sons and seven daughters.

Pop's host, the overall factory owner took him home with him for a reason, because he had an ulterior motive. He was a very smart man. He saw an eligible bachelor and he was trying to find a husband for one of his seven daughters. Pop fell for it. The girls were all fashionably dressed and fancy Bostonian ladies. Pop started making frequent bus trips to Boston to buy merchandise and to see Rose, the prettiest one. They found they had a lot in common. They loved to go dancing and waltz to their favorite song, "By the Light of the Silvery Moon". Pop proposed and they were married in a beautiful garden wedding in Boston on June 1st, 1915. After a short honeymoon, they went back to Maine to live. Their first child, my brother, Daniel, was born on March 1st, 1916, exactly nine months to the day after they wed. Some of our relatives teased pop and called him "Sure Shot Harry". Years later, I thought it was because he was a good basketball player, but that was not the reason, although he did love to play basketball at the "Y". My sister, Lillian, was born in Maine in October of 1921 6 ½ years later. So, my brother and sister were both born in Maine.

CHAPTER **2**

MY MOTHER HAD always been close to her biological brother and two real sisters, not the stepsisters and half-sisters and half-brothers. Her oldest sister, Katie, was married, had a son and a daughter. She still lived in Boston. Her other sister, Hannah, was married and had six children. Hannah's husband came from a good family, but he was an alcoholic and could not keep a job. He had no ambition and was not much of a worker. They had six children together that she raised alone. Therefore, Hannah was the breadwinner. Her two oldest children were finishing high school and very intelligent and started applying to Colleges. The oldest one won a scholarship and wanted to attend Syracuse University. So, aunt Hannah and her family moved to Syracuse. My mother missed her beloved sister, Hannah, and became depressed. Pop sold his store in Maine and they moved to Syracuse, NY too, so she could be near Hannah. Pop opened a shoe store. I was born in June of 1927 in the Good

Shepherd Hospital, which later became part of Syracuse University upstate medical school. We lived in an apartment behind the shoe store and pop's business was thriving. He made money and invested it in stocks. Every Friday night we had dinner with aunt Hannah and her family. We were close.

In 1929, the great depression came. That changed our life. Nobody had any money for shoes and there was no money for rent. Pop lost his business, the banks closed and the money he had was gone and the Stocks he had invested in were worthless. Then my mother became sick. I was only two when we had to move back to my grandfather's House in Boston. My mother passed away and pop had no job or way to take care of us. Then my grandfather passed away and we couldn't live there anymore because his wife was not our real grandmother. I was so young when I lost my mother that the only things I remember about her was that she always gave me water to drink instead of milk. Also, when she dressed me she said, "all dressed up and no place to go". My poor pop had no wife, no place to live and three children to raise. My aunts came to the rescue. Daniel was almost fifteen and in high school so aunt Katie took him to live with her until he finished school in Boston. Pop took me back to Syracuse on the train to live with aunt Hannah. Then he and Lillian returned to Maine to stay in Lewiston at Aunt Mary's. Pop was able to get a job in a shoe factory. At one time, he worked for L.L. Bean making boots. He was very unhappy about his three children being separated and living in different states with different aunts. He was a good father but had very bad luck. During the time we lived in Boston, my sister, Lil, taught me how to read when I was about three years old, I guess that's where I got my love for reading. When I started school, I skipped first grade and they put me in second grade. I was always the youngest kid in my class.

CHAPTER **3**

TWO OF AUNT Hannah's kids had graduated from college by the time I came to live with them in Syracuse. She treated me like I was her own. Her kids were a lot older than I was, but they played with me and were like big sisters and brothers to me. Besides her own, she had a college student as a boarder by the name of Horace. At first I thought pop said a horse lived there and was confused! I wondered how a horse could live in an upstairs city apartment. The oldest daughter, Delia, graduated, moved to New York city and got a good job. The oldest son, Lou, graduated from law school, passed the bar, and was brilliant. He started his own law office. The next three were in college and had nicknames. They were "Tootsie", "Chick" and "Pikey". The youngest daughter whose nickname was "Bubbles" was still in high school. I wanted to show them that I could read so I took the mail out of the Mailbox and read Delia's typed letters to the neighbors and then the family. I was showing off reading personal mail to strangers. I couldn't understand why aunt Hannah scolded me, saying I was bad.

There's always one mischievous one in every family and it was Chick, the middle guy. He bought an old car and wanted an adventure. A couple of his college buddies and their girlfriends went for a ride with him to northern New York and crossed the bridge to Canada. When the girls didn't come home when they were supposed to, the worried mothers called the police and reported them missing. They were Caught, brought back to Syracuse, thrown in jail, and the guys were charged with illegally leaving the country with female minors. They were bailed out of jail. A court hearing date was set. When it came to court, the judge told Chick he could sentence him to twenty years in jail for this offense. He was a cocky young kid. His brother Lou, who was his attorney, was going to tell the court that it was his first offense and they were only college kids going on a harmless joyride. Before Lou could say anything, Chick opened his big smart-mouth and said, "go ahead". The judge banged his gavel and said, "I sentence you to twenty years". And Chick went to jail. There was nothing Lou could do. Aunt Hannah cried her eyes out. There was a lot of bad publicity and Lou had to close his law office because he wasn't getting any clients. He couldn't even afford the office rent. Hannah's husband was an alcoholic and couldn't hold a job. She was the main breadwinner. She had supported the family earning money by bootlegging, making moonshine (illegal booze) to finance her children's college education and support the family.

When Prohibition ended in 1933, so did her income. By then, her daughter, Tootsie, was a graduate dietitian and was offered jobs in hospitals. Pikey, who was around twenty years old, dropped out of college because all the kids teased him about his brother being a jailbird. It was shameful and embarrassing living in Syracuse. They bought an old truck and packed everything up and moved to Ogdensburg, NY, a small town on the St. Lawrence river in northern New York. Of course, I moved with them, and that is where I grew up.

CHAPTER 4

AUNT HANNAH RENTED a large old house with a big barn in Ogdensburg. She became a junk dealer. She found out how much junk was worth. She had a large scale in the barn and people brought their old rags and metal, which they were glad to get rid of. She paid for them by the pound. When she had a large quantity, a wholesale junk dealer would come in a horse and buggy and buy them from her and that's how she earned a living. Pikey got a job and contributed, too. My pop worked in Maine in a shoe factory and saved enough money to come to Ogdensburg to visit us. It was a small northern NY town. Aunt Hannah introduced him to a lot of people. He wanted to meet someone to marry, to make a home for his three children, so we could all be together again.

He met a single lady around his age by the name of Kassie Baker. Her first husband had deserted her. She was divorced and seemed nice enough. He married her, and she became our stepmother. She had a grown son from her unhappy short previous marriage. He lived with her parents, his grandparents. He couldn't get along with his own mother, so refused to live with her. We soon found out why. She wasn't very motherly, even to him. She was mean, stingy, and nasty and turned out to be the "proverbial wicked stepmother". She was only nice to us when pop was around. She was a good actress and pretended to like us but really didn't. If she sent me to the store to buy a loaf of wonder bread which cost nine cents, and gave me a dime to pay for it, she would holler after me to bring home the penny change. All the kids on the block would mimic "bring the witch home the penny change." How embarrassing!

to my aunt Hannah's house and stay there until pop would come and get me and make me come home I didn't want to go home with Kassie. She was mean and stingy.

In New York, it snowed a lot. On the snow days when there was no school I went to my aunt Hannah's. She would bring in some new, clean white snow and pour Hershey's syrup on it for a treat sometimes. She taught me how to knit using lollipop sticks for knitting needles. She was a great cook and baker and there was always good food. I was always welcome to come over. She was a big influence on my life. I loved school and skipped another grade, so I started high school when I was only thirteen. Again, I was the youngest kid in my class. I took commercial courses and learned shorthand, typing, and accounting and business subjects. Also, the basic math, English and science. While I was in high school, the war started and a program was set up to raise money to fight the war by selling government war bonds. The kids in school would save until they got $18.75, the price of a twenty-five-dollar war bond. I was honest and smart and trusted. I was chosen to collect the money, deposit it in the bank, keep track of it. I gave receipts to the students as I collected the funds. Then I had to type the bond forms with the purchaser's names and information. The manager of the movie theater oversaw our war bond fund program. I would go to his office to type the bonds after school and then distribute them in school the following day. Not only did I contribute to the war effort, I got to see all the movies free!

CHAPTER **6**

WHEN LIL TURNED sixteen we had a big party for her. Our cousin Pikey drove his sister Bubbles to our house. Aunt Hannah sent the birthday cake and other goodies she had baked and cooked especially for the party. Lil's girlfriends were all invited. When Pikey saw Lil's best friend, Margaret who was a very beautiful sixteen-year-old girl, it was love at first sight. They started dating. They eloped and got married a couple of years later. Bubbles graduated from high school and entered a nursing program in New York city. Aunt Hannah's kids were all grown and gone now, so she kicked her useless drunken husband out of the house for the final time, I was there like I usually was most of the time. She was mopping her kitchen floor one morning when he came banging on the locked screen door screaming obscenities at her and yelling for her to open-up and let him in. She threw the pail of dirty mop water through the screen at him. She told him to get lost and never come back. The following winter he was intoxicated and slipped on the ice and split his head open and died. She did not even go to his funeral, saying she wasn't a hypocrite.

Aunt Hannah was now living all alone in her big house. Pikey and Margaret were married and had their own house. Margaret loved her mother-in-law, Hannah, as soon as she met her. Pikey and Margaret didn't want her to live alone, so they asked her to come and live with them. Margaret's own mother had abandoned her when she was a little girl. She knew what a sweet, wonderful person and marvelous cook Hannah was. Aunt Hannah thanked them but refused when Margaret first asked her. But when she got pregnant Hannah gave in. She knew she could help Margaret who was still working, and after the baby was born. She took most of her furniture with her and all her valuables. She closed her junkyard and got rid of her big, old, drafty house and she moved in with them. Pikey was in "heaven" because he had the two women he loved living with him. He knew his mom would be a big help and loving grandma.

CHAPTER 7

ON DECEMBER SEVENTH, 1941, President Roosevelt declared war. All eligible males who were physically able who were eighteen years and older had to register for selective service. Lillian's boyfriend and Pikey were among the first to be drafted and had to go to war with the other young guys who became "The Greatest Generation". There was no school the day they left Ogdensburg on the train for basic training. The whole town went to the train station to see them off. Many of them were only kids. They were not wanting to go and leaning out of the open train windows and hollering goodbyes and throwing kisses to everyone. Parents, girlfriends, neighbors and everyone cried. They knew they were going to war and might not be coming back. My high school started a new accelerated program so the senior boys who were nearing the age to be drafted (when they turned eighteen), could finish high school, graduate, and get their diploma before they too, had to leave to go in the service.

It was 1943 and the beginning of my Senior year when tragedy struck my family. Lil's boyfriend, who had been drafted early in the war, was sent to an army base in the south for basic training. Lil went there and they were married. As soon as he completed basic training her hubby was sent overseas. Lil came back to Ogdensburg and lived with his sister, her sister-in-law, Anita. Shortly thereafter he was killed in the north African invasion with general Montgomery's ground forces. He was sent home in a casket, escorted by officers from his unit and he had a military funeral with a twenty-one-gun salute. Lil fainted. She was a young widow and she was devastated. I was too upset to attend school and stayed with her for a week. Margaret and Pikey's baby arrived. He was a few months old at the time when Pikey had to leave too. After training he was sent overseas. He was wounded and returned to Walter Reed hospital in Washington DC, where he passed away.

His body was returned to Ogdensburg. I had another funeral to attend plus I had to babysit while Margaret and my aunt Hannah took care of funeral arrangements and all the other things, poor aunt Hannah and Margaret! I missed more school. Of course, the obituaries appeared in "the Ogdensburg Advance News", the local newspaper, along with the other casualties. When I finally returned to school, after missing two weeks during a very short time. I had a note excusing my absence. On my first day back, my social science teacher, Mr. Getman, accused me of playing hooky and skipping school, he said I was a truant. I tried to explain to him what happened and that my brother-in-law and my first cousin were killed and I had to attend funerals of two relatives. He called me a liar and I called him a Nazi. He was very angry and I got scared and I really thought he was going to hit me. I ran out of his class and down the hall. He chased me all the way to the principal's office who asked what all the commotion was about. He told the teacher, Mr. Getman, to go back to his class and told me from now on to come to his office every day instead of going to that class for that period.

The principal had a side business nobody knew about. He was raising white mice for laboratory experiments and selling them to labs all over the country. His secretary was too busy to write letters and take orders for white mice on school time. I did whatever they needed in their office, as long as I didn't have to go back to Mr. Getman's class. So, during that period I took orders and arranged to ship white mice and bill for them. Some days I did that. On other days, I worked on the new accelerated program for the boys to graduate early who were nearing draft age. I had to research each male's records and check their birthdays to determine who was nearing draft age. I was the only girl who got into that program. I graduated in January when the boys did, six months early, and I received a diploma. Then I came back the following June to graduate and walk with the rest of my class. I have two high school diplomas. While I was in high school I worked at Woolworth's 5 & 10 cent store part-time. Between the war fund bond project and school homework and a part-time weekend job, I was a busy teenager.

CHAPTER **8**

I WAS FINISHED with high school, there was no money for college, and no jobs available in Ogdensburg. I begged my father to let me go to Washington, DC to work for the FBI. I had passed the test when a recruiter came to my school and tested the senior girls. I had a government job waiting, but he didn't want me to go alone because I was only sixteen. I asked if I could go to New York city. Pop said he would see if he could make arrangements with a cousin there. Pop once again had a small men's clothing store. He was going to New York to buy merchandise for his store. He had several cousins who lived in the Bronx and Brooklyn, New York. He always saw them when he went there. He told his cousin, Sadie, who lived in Brooklyn, how much I was begging him to go to New York and what a good kid I was, she said "send her here and she can stay with us." Her two sons were away in the service and she only had her grown daughter, Pauline, living at home. She had plenty of room. Now I had to figure out how to get there.

The husband of one of my sister Lillian's friends had been wounded overseas and sent to an army hospital in Staten Island. She asked my Sister, Lil, if she would go with her to NY so she wouldn't have to go alone. I always used to tag along behind Lil, so I asked her if I could go, too. Pop said it would be okay if I went with them. They were going by train from Ogdensburg to New York city. I went along on the train. We stayed in a hotel in Manhattan overnight. The next day they took me to Brooklyn by subway to pop's cousin Sadie's house and left me there. I never told anybody how scared I was and that I cried myself to sleep every night for the first couple of weeks I was there, even though Sadie and her husband Jake were very nice to me.

CHAPTER **9**

JAKE, TAUGHT ME how to get around by subway. He had a nephew who managed a business in downtown Brooklyn making precision scientific instruments like hydrometers, hygrometers, and other testing equipment such as huge commercial industrial thermometers. He happened to need office help. Jake took me there and his nephew liked me and hired me. The first day I worked there the boss asked me to get Greiner on the phone. I had no idea who Greiner was or how to call him. That's when I found out I wasn't very smart.

In Ogdensburg when you wanted to make a phone call all you had to do was pick up the receiver and the operator said, "number please". If you didn't know it she would get it for you. I had never seen a dial phone before or used a telephone book. The NYC phone directory was huge. Lucky for me, a delivery man walked into the office and saw I was a new young girl. He showed me how to look up the number in the telephone directory and use a dial telephone for the very first time. The boss who was in his back office was wondering what was Taking so long. He just assumed the line was busy. It didn't take me long to learn how to run that office. I was underpaid but I worked There for two years. I lived with Sadie and Jake for a couple of months. I paid them ten dollars per week so I could manage on my small salary.

CHAPTER **10**

SOMEBODY TOLD ME there was a girls' club in Brooklyn near prospect park where there were eighty-five girls living. When I went there, they had no vacancies. I had to fill out an application, give references and wait for the next opening. The only time a girl left was when she got married or moved back to her old home town. Some of the girls living there were trying to get in show business on Broadway, some attended college, and others were pursuing careers in the big apple. All the girls living there loved it, despite the strict rules. No guys were allowed upstairs. Every night they had bed check after curfew, which was at ten pm. Mrs. Murphy was the housekeeper who enforced the rules. Every night she went to every room to check and make sure all the girls were in. Then she would lock the front door. If you were not in by bed check time more than once you got kicked out.

Breakfast and dinner were provided. We had to

turn in our war ration coupons so there would be enough food. It took most of my paycheck to live there, but it was worth it. We celebrated all the holidays. Every Saturday night we had a USO party and dance. We had a conga line that everybody joined in. Such fun! The Brooklyn navy yard was only a trolley car ride away and servicemen rode free. There were always sailors around, especially one by the name of Dewey. When a new girl came, he would introduce himself and befriend her. I was warned that he tried to get every girl to go to bed with him, so I was prepared to give him the brushoff. The girls club had a huge kitchen, dining room and two gigantic beautifully furnished living rooms downstairs. They got lots of use. Dormitory bedrooms were upstairs and off-limits unless you resided there. Guys were not allowed upstairs. There were nice bathrooms on every floor with several tile showers and a separate laundry room with washers and clotheslines (because there were no dryers back then) and ironing boards. There were pay telephones in the hallways to make and receive calls. There were strict rules, like a ten o'clock curfew and no horseplay or cussing allowed.

As soon as they contacted me and said a room was available I told cousin Sadie. I thanked them for their hospitality and moved to the girls' club. I had four room-mates who were all different, but all nice, and I had Friends for the first time since leaving

Ogdensburg. My roommate from Winnipeg, Canada, wanted to be a photographer, took pictures of anything and everything. She had to set up an elaborate system for lighting. One Thanksgiving she blew up the electricity and we were unable to have a turkey dinner. We had cold sandwiches instead. We listened to the radio, played board games, shopped, went to prospect park, went sight-seeing all over New York city and had fun. I no longer cried myself to sleep missing my family and friends back home in Ogdensburg.

CHAPTER 11

ON D-DAY, JUNE 6, 1944, when U.S. troops entered France and an important operation was planned to end the war, we heard on the radio that exciting things were happening in Times Square in Manhattan. Some of the girls invited me to go with them by subway to see what was happening. When we came up the stairs from the subway to times square, there were crowds of servicemen everywhere. They grabbed us and started kissing and hugging us. I was not quite seventeen years old yet and I got scared, turned around and took the subway back to Brooklyn. That's the day the famous picture was taken of a service man kissing a young girl that was in all the papers and magazines.

I kept in touch with cousin Sadie. We called each other and she invited me to dinner or to go to Long Island with them for the weekend to "the farm", a summer house the three sisters had. All the relatives Congregated there at different times. Kid cousin,

Jackie, would come with his parents, Gussie and Joe, and entertain us. In September 1945, Sadie called me at the girls' club. She said her sons were being discharged and coming home from the service, along with her neighbors' sons. They were planning a big block party to welcome them home. They planned to bring out card tables, radios with extension cords, and bake lots of goodies and have drinks. They needed girls for the fellows to dance with. Sadie asked me to bring some girls from the girls' club and come to their neighborhood welcome home party. I invited my room-mates. One of the girls, Jean, was about ten years older than me and I thought she would be perfect for Sadie's sons, who were in their thirties. But neither one was interested in her. They all went for the young chicks. It was a great block party, everybody had fun.

That's where I first met Al and my life changed. He was so handsome and immediately took a liking to me, even though I was only eighteen and he was thirty-four. He stuck to me like glue. We had to be back at the Girls club by ten pm. He escorted us back by trolley car. On the way he told us about being a tail gunner in a B-26 bomber during the war. He took us to our door and then went home. He called me at the office the following day and asked me if he could see me after work. He didn't have to ask me twice. I was so flattered and excited. I thought the day would never end. He was waiting in front of the building when I came out and we took the subway to Manhattan. We ate at the H & H Automat and then he took me to Grand Central Station, the train terminal, where we could sit and talk. There Were lots of people there but I didn't see any of them, only Al!

CHAPTER **12**

AL TOLD ME about growing up in Brooklyn. Danny Kaye was one of his high school classmates and the class clown. Al was fascinated with Airplanes and wanted to go into aeronautics, but his parents objected. His mom said only a crazy person would fly up in the air. He used to go out to Floyd Bennett field and wash airplanes so they would take Him up for a ride in one of the small planes. His dad paid for and made him go to an automotive mechanics' school, after which he opened a Shell gas station with a partner. He had violin lessons when he was growing up and played well. But he always wanted to learn how to play the trumpet. He bought one and taught himself how to play. When he had no customers in his gas station, he played his trumpet.

He wanted to buy a motorcycle, but his parents said it was too dangerous. His favorite aunt told him to buy one, anyway, and he could Keep it at her house, a couple of blocks away. He was riding it one day and had to stop at a red light and there were his parents, ready to cross the street. They caught him, and after that he kept it at home. He bought a side-car and took his relatives for rides. He had it for awhile and his young brother kept pestering him for rides. Then his brother asked him to teach him how to drive it. Al got in the side-car and they took off. They went around the block and as they turned the corner the kid lost control and they crashed into the house on the corner. It happened to be the home of the Postmaster-general of New York city. They came through the picture window of the dining room, without being invited to dinner. The kid jumped off the motorcycle and left Al sitting in the side-car. Luckily, nobody got hurt, but Al had to pay for the damage. That was the end of the ruined motorcycle.

His stories were so fascinating that we lost track of the time. The big clock in Grand Central showed that it was getting late. I knew I would never make it back to the girls' club by ten pm curfew so I called my roommates and asked them to fix my bed with pillows and blankets and make it look like I was asleep. They turned off the lights and told Mrs. Murphy to be quiet when she came to do her nightly bed check. Al brought me back at five am so I could sneak back in when the milkman came to deliver milk. I couldn't go to work wearing the same clothes as the day before, so I showered, dressed, and went to work without going to bed.

I only did that one other time, but prepared the girls ahead of time to cover for me. Al had invited me on a real date to go to Lou Walters Latin quarters night club for dinner, the extravagant show, and dancing. I went shopping and bought a beautiful expensive dress and new fancy shoes. When I looked in the mirror I couldn't believe it was me. I knew there was no way I could be back by 10 pm. I am not usually a sneaky person, but we were falling in love. I had my first drink that night. It was a Tom Collins, and after a couple of them we danced until the place closed at 2 am. Again, I sneaked in with the milkman at 5 am, but the next day was Sunday and I could sleep in.

CHAPTER **13**

ON SUNDAY MORNING Al's mother Sadie asked him where he had been all night and he told her the truth. She told him to stop seeing me because we were third cousins and I was too young. He said he had lots of girlfriends before, several in Europe, as well as in Brooklyn before the war, but never felt like this about any of them. She said there were plenty of other girls in New York. He told her I was really special, sweet and innocent and he was in love with me. She said she liked me but I was a distant cousin, and I was only a snot-nose kid. She got upset with him and had a big argument. He stormed out of the house. Al continued calling me at the office and the boss told him to stop. When Al found out I was only making $20 a week he said I should ask for a raise. I finally got enough courage to ask for a raise. The boss asked when I was leaving. I said I wasn't intending to leave but if that was his answer I was giving him two weeks' notice. I told him to hire someone and I would train her. He never did and I left after the two weeks. Afterward, I heard from one of the glass-blowers who worked there that he had to hire two people to do my job, a book-keeper and a secretary. I bought the N.Y. times newspaper and started job hunting.

The first ad I answered was for a secretary in a garment factory. The owner got fresh with me so I told him off and left. The next ad was with the Bulova Watch Company on the 37th floor of theInternational Bldg. in Rockefeller Center. The Personnel manager asked why I left my last job and hired Me immediately at a starting salary of $40. A week. I was the Secretary to a gentleman who had to answer all the letters from customers who were having problems with their watches. Usually we would just send a form letter telling them how to Fix the problem. Some of them required a letter so they could replace it if necessary. This boss loved my letters and we had a good relationship. My only problem was that my desk was near the window and if I looked out, I got dizzy. The Radio City Rockettes worked out and rehearsed on the roof of Radio City Music Hall and you could see them from the window. Another girl was very happy to switch desks with me. The office manager asked me if I would work for a different Boss while his secretary went on vacation. He was the director of public relations. We got along great. When his old Secretary did not come back, he asked me to work for him Permanently and got me

a raise. So, I was promoted. My boss at Bulova contacted General Omar Bradley. They arranged to start
a watch repair school for war Veterans in Long Island
City, NY. I did a lot of the secretarial work for that. I
asked Al if he would like to attend but he was only
interested in working with airplanes, not watches.

CHAPTER 14

DESPITE HIS PARENTS' objections and other obstacles, Al continued dating me. He was looking for the right job. He decided to go after his dream and become a pilot. He sent applications to the schools accepting the G.I. bill for Veterans and was accepted at Peter's Flying school in Ithaca, NY. My cousin Pikey's widow, Margaret, was now living in Ithaca and I wrote and told her about Al. She found him a place to live and made it possible for him to start. Some of the classes were at Cornell university for navigation, meteorology, etc. The actual training field where they learned to fly and had instructors was at Peter's airfield. Al loved it but he had a problem with depth perception and was trying to work it out.

Al missed me and asked me to come to Ithaca and marry him. My pop and his parents all objected to us getting married, so we decided to elope. We didn't need a big, fancy wedding. We just needed each other. I gave notice to my boss at the Bulova Watch company and the girls club and took the greyhound bus to Ithaca where Al and Margaret were awaiting my arrival. Margaret made all the arrangements with Hillel at Cornell for us to be married. After Pikey's death she moved to Ithaca and started a new life with her little son. My aunt Hannah went to live with her daughter in Boston. Neither one of them wanted to stay in Ogdensburg.

Margaret got a job in a fancy-dress shop, made new friends, including the mayor of Ithaca, and a young couple who were foot doctors. The wife was a chiropodist and the husband was a podiatrist. They had met in college, married, and opened a practice in the First National Bank building in Ithaca. Margaret introduced us to them and they agreed to be our witnesses at our wedding. I bought a pretty sexy new dress (not a wedding gown) in the store where Margaret worked and Al had a gardenia bouquet for me. He had been living in a rented room in a private home. Until we could find something else, I went there temporarily.

CHAPTER **15**

AFTER THE WEDDING, Margaret and her boyfriend, who was the Mayor of Ithaca, and the doctor couple took us out for dinner and drinks. We went back to Al's room temporarily. The next day we went looking for an apartment to rent near downtown, where we found a small affordable apartment. We, were in love, but it was impossible to live on Al's income of the Fifty-Two Twenty Club ($20 per week for 52 weeks). So, I had to get a job. I found a job working for the Cornell Daily Sun, the Cornell University newspaper. The editor was a college student studying journalism. He came to the office after class and I was his secretary. I did his typing for him in the afternoons. Mornings I took the classified ads for the paper, some on the phone and some in person. I did not make as much money as I had in NYC, but I had some savings and things were cheaper in Ithaca.

One of the classified ads I took was for a used car.

It was a 1926 Nash that had been stored in a barn in Horseheads, NY for years. Al got a ride to Horseheads to look it over. It had window shades that could be pulled up and down. It ran but the black paint was all faded and ugly. Al bought it for $65, he did some repairs so it would run better. He tuned it up, and painted it a bright green. I named it Kelly. All the college kids wanted to buy it from him. One weekend we went from Ithaca to NYC, on the way the fan belt broke, we went to a small store in a village in the mountains and Al bought a clothesline which he braided and used instead. His ingenuity got us there and back over a long weekend. It was still on there when we finally sold the old car.

CHAPTER **16**

AL WAS DOING well with his classes at Cornell, and learning to fly at the airfield. However, he had a problem landing. He broke the struts and landing gear on a couple of the single engine piper club training planes because of his lack of depth perception. The owner of the flying school, Mr. Peters, called him into his office. He told him unfortunately he would never become a pilot. Mr. Peters knew of his love of Aviation and that he was mechanically inclined. He recommended that he study aircraft instruments. He told him that there was a school called "West Coast University School of Aircraft Instruments" which was accredited and approved for Veterans. He advised him to apply. The only problem was that it was in California.

When we got the newspaper the following day, we were shocked to read the headlines. There had been a tragic accident. Our friends, the doctor couple, had left their office in the bank building, pressed the elevator button, the elevator door opened, but when they stepped in, the elevator was not there. They fell four stories down to the basement of the bank and were killed instantly. We were devastated. They had become very good friends. Al was not going to be able to continue at flying school. Our new friends were gone, and we felt like it was time to leave Ithaca and move on. I gave my notice to the manager of the "Cornell Daily Sun" after being there a year. We found a couple to take our apartment, and sold our car to a Cornell student for the same $65 we paid for it. When we told Margaret, we were leaving she couldn't stop crying. We packed up our personal belongings and went back to Brooklyn. While we were in Ithaca, we had written and called Al's parents and they finally accepted me. Now, I was their daughter-in-law as well as a relative. Al applied for admission to "West Coast University" and was accepted. We had to find a way to California, but didn't have much money. We were living on love!

Al purchased "The New York Times" paper and saw an ad in the classified personnel section from a gentleman who needed someone to drive his new car from New York to Los Angeles. This was in 1947 when it was almost impossible to buy a new car. This man was an executive with Federated Department stores. He was being transferred from Macy's in New York to Burdines in Los Angeles and did not have time to drive his car cross-country. We called the phone number in the ad and were told to meet the man in a hotel in Manhattan. There were two other people there when we arrived. One was an Englishman who wanted to see the United States and the Other was a twenty-something young girl who had to return to California to take care of her sick mother. Al suggested we all go together, which the owner of the car thought was a great idea. We showed him our drivers licenses, other identification, references, and signed some papers. He gave Al the car keys and we arranged to pick up our companions and their belongings.

CHAPTER **17**

THE FOLLOWING DAY we started our journey. Al drove first because he knew his way around New York and the best way to get on the shortcut out of the city and to the highway where we could follow our map. The two guys sat in the front and the other girl sat in the back seat with me. There was so much luggage for four people that it wouldn't all fit in the trunk, so the extra luggage was in the back seat with us. Every time we went around a curve, the suitcases would fall over and squash us. After a couple of hours, the British man said he would like to drive, so they switched seats. First, he started driving on the wrong side of the road, like they do in England. Then he started speeding going eighty miles per hour. Al told him to slow down or we would get a ticket. He answered that the speedometer went up to one hundred fifty, so he would just outrun the police. Al told him the cops would shoot the tires and to just obey the speed limit.

As we were riding, he started telling us how much money he made in England dealing in the black market. He also had schemes to make money illegally in the U.S. because Americans are so "naive and dumb". We just listened quietly. They took turns driving now that Al told him the rules. We drove until it started to get dark the first day and got to Kentucky. We stopped at a motel for the night where there was a restaurant and cabins. After dinner, Al and I knocked on the girl's cabin door and told her we planned to leave the next morning at six am, not at seven am like the Englishman said. Early the following morning Al took all the other man's luggage out of the car and left it in on the front porch of his cabin door. We left at six am, not seven. We drove off and abandoned him and his get-rich- schemes in Kentucky. Now all the luggage fit in the trunk and the three of us were more comfortable.

Along the way, we stopped and picked cotton in a cotton field, visited the Alamo in Texas, and took in all the sights and enjoyed our beautiful America. The only problem we had was when we got to the desert in Arizona where the car overheated and we stopped. The girl said it was a good thing Al knew what to do. We waited for it to cool off, added coolant to the radiator, and could continue. It took us a week to drive to California and the owner said we could keep the car for another week to get settled before delivering it to him. We took the girl to her mother's house in Beverly Hills and started looking for a place to live. We found a rooming house where we had kitchen privileges on a side street near Wilshire Blvd. The elderly couple who owned it were very nice.

We met a young couple who lived there and we became friends. Jerry was a musician and played first violin with the Los Angeles Philharmonic Orchestra. She was taking music lessons and hoped to become an opera star. Jerry took us car shopping. We went to "Honest John's" used car lot on Wilshire Blvd. and Al bought a cheap used Chevrolet for $265. Which was all we could afford. Then we delivered the new car we had driven from NY to Burdines to its owner who was delighted. The used car Al bought broke down right after we bought it. But Honest John was dishonest, wouldn't take it back. Luckily, Al was able to fix it enough to drive it and we were stuck with it. It got us around, but we had to plan ahead to make a turn because the steering system didn't work. Al got a job in a gas station until the next class started at West Coast University. I got a job as a secretary with a wholesale cosmetics firm and learned how to get there by bus. After about a month I started to feel sick. I thought perhaps it was because of the change in water or because we were eating out a lot. But every morning I was throwing up. I barely made it on the bus to my new job. I told my landlady and she said I must be pregnant (and I was!). She said as much as she loved babies, and liked us we couldn't stay there after I had the baby.

CHAPTER **18**

WHILE WE WERE on our journey to California in October of 1947 we drove between eight and ten hours per day and stayed in a hotel or motel where we made love every night. We hadn't had a honeymoon before so this was it!!! That's when I must have conceived. We started looking for an apartment. Some were too expensive and others were too far away from a bus line and we only had one car. We finally found a place that allowed children that we could afford. It was in a building that had four apartments, two downstairs and two upstairs. Ours was upstairs above the owner's' apartment. It was nicely furnished, located a block away from Sunset Boulevard on Micheltorena street in Hollywood, right near a bus stop. Saul, our landlord, was a war veteran, too. He and Al had a lot in common. He owned a radio repair shop and when television started he got one of the first T.V.'s. Louise, his wife, was a little older than me and a lovely person. They had a baby who was around a year and a half old and she was pregnant again. She recommended her OB-GYN, but he was too expensive, so I found a general practitioner I really liked and he took good care of my prenatal needs. He used a small hospital by the name of Madison Hospital in Hollywood for his deliveries. Some of the movie stars went there because it was more private. I worked as-long-as I could. My boss at the office understood when I gave notice that I was leaving because it was pretty obvious I had a tummy bump.

Al started classes at West Coast University. He loved working on aircraft instruments and new electronics. Every evening we went downstairs and visited with our landlord, Saul, and Louise. While we talked, Al started telling stories about his amazing war experiences. We watched their small TV. The picture was snowy and mostly wrestling was on. Al said before he enlisted he bought a new car on his thirtieth birthday. It was a Pontiac which he paid $1,004.62 for, including license plates, taxes and everything. While he was away, his parents sold it to a relative for the same price he paid, thinking he could buy another one when he came home. His parents needed and used the money. But after the war new cars were not available or affordable so he couldn't get one.

CHAPTER 19

ONE OF THE stories Al told Saul was that in 1942, after his kid brother was drafted in the army, he enlisted
in the Air Corps. He was sent for training as a tail gunner with the 454th bomb squadron to Macdill field
in Tampa. Then, for further training in Miami Beach,
where his unit was billeted in the Flamingo Hotel until they were shipped to England. They arrived before
all the planes. They flew B-26 whitetail marauder airplanes on dangerous missions over Germany flying
low and skip-bombing targets. One by one they were
shot down and sometimes returned to base "on a wing
and a prayer". The day before the last plane flew, the
crew was given inoculations. Al had a bad reaction
and was running a fever so he was left behind in bed.
He wouldn't have been alive now because that plane
was shot down and that was the end of B-26 whitetail
marauders. Now he was left without a unit and there
are no more B-26 whitetail marauder planes. Before
the war, Al operated a gas station and could keep

inventory and account for every item. They needed a PX manager and since he had no unit and he had merchandising experience he was then appointed PX manager for his base in England.

They were preparing for the Battle of The Bulge and the Normandy invasion. He was told to pack up his PX and have everything loaded on a ship that was waiting, but he wasn't told when the ship was departing to cross the English Channel. There was a mix-up and he got left behind. He was separated from his unit and wound up crossing on a different smaller boat. He ended up wading to shore all muddy and exhausted. Finally, he found his unit and his jeep and could set up his PX. After that France was invaded. Besides being first in England he was also in Ardennes, Normandy, northern France, central Europe and Rhineland. Their air offensive gave support to General Patton's ground war. As the troops moved forward, Al had to move the PX with them.

Shortly after the Germans surrendered, Al's commanding officer came into the PX and asked him if he knew how to speak German. He informed him he was looking for someone for a special assignment to go to the holocaust horrible concentration camp, Dachau, which was being liberated and take goodies to the prisoners. Al loaded the jeep with candy bars, crackers, cookies, cigarettes, etc. They opened the big gates to Dachau and Al drove his jeep in first. He told them he was an American who came to set them free. As he was handing out the goodies, the prisoners started falling and passing away in front of him. They were like walking skeletons. There were piles of clothes and the smoke from the gas chambers was still spewing the stench of human flesh burning in the air. There is a video of this which can be seen in Washington, D.C. at the holocaust museum. This was the first-time Al ever spoke about this horrible experience. Our land-lord, Saul, said his job in the service was in communications and the main thing he had to do was keep the radio equipment operating on the bases and in the planes.

CHAPTER **20**

AFTER THE WAR, Saul went back to repairing radios. The television industry was starting and Saul said he wanted to start stocking and selling T.V.'s and get in on the ground floor. He had the shop for T.V.'s, but he didn't have the money. He decided to sell the four-apartment house we lived in so he would have the cash he needed to invest in T.V.'s and become an authorized RCA dealer. At that same time, I had to go on maternity leave. I was worried how we would manage without my salary. The new owner of the house was an older gentleman. He had a daughter who was a single parent. They moved into the other apartment upstairs next to us. He reduced our rent and paid me to babysit his darling little grandchild. Now our former landlord was a tenant just like we were and we could afford it. Al continued his education in Glendale at West Coast University and I stayed home. On July 15th, 1948, I started having labor pains. When Al came home he took me to the hospital. After a long, hard labor our first son was born on July 16th. I named him Richard after my mother. Like most babies, he cried a lot. I discovered he would stop crying if I vacuumed, so we had a very clean apartment.

While we were living out there we had one of those scary famous earthquakes. The Crib was on wheels and started rolling back and forth across the bedroom floor. Ricky (Richard) thought we were playing with him and laughed and laughed. Ricky loved playing with his dad Al's war medals. I have no idea where the medals are now. We had a Taylor-tot stroller with a basket on the back. Our little Pekingese dog Chinky would ride in the basket and we would walk to a little park where Sunset, Vine and Hollywood Blvd.'s all met. When I went to the supermarket I would leave Chinky home and pack the groceries in the basket.

CHAPTER **21**

MY SISTER, LIL, and I corresponded with each other and kept in touch. She lived with her sister-in-law, Anita, and Anita's husband, Clarence Leduc, and she worked as a long-distance operator for the phone company. She went bowling with her girlfriends and met a great guy who came back to Ogdensburg after the war when he was discharged from the service. They started dating. Anita didn't like the idea, but Lil didn't care. She accepted later when he finally proposed to her. We met Jim just before we moved to California. They were married in October of 1946 in a small wedding. He worked for a customs brokerage firm and was transferred from Ogdensburg to the bridge at Alexandria bay, so they moved to the bay. Lil transferred with the telephone company too, first they rented an apartment and then they bought a large house. They lived in the apartment until Lil got pregnant. The apartment was fine for the two of them, but not large enough for the family they planned to have, so they bought a large house on Bolton avenue.

Lil left her job with the telephone company and stayed home. They had to buy new furniture and decorate the house and prepare for the arrival of their new baby. Lil went into a long labor on a cold day in Dec. 1947 and Just before midnight on December 10th, 1947 She gave birth to their first son, Bobby, in the small Hospital in Alexandria bay, NY. She didn't know she was having twins, but she was still having labor pains after the first one was born. They sent her by ambulance to Watertown, NY, to a larger hospital. She made newspaper headlines when she delivered twin brother, Johnny, in Watertown over 18 hours later, on December 11, 1947. Jim was a big help and great dad. Over the next fifteen years she had five more kids. I love them all -- my one niece and all six of my Nephews.

We were always close although we lived far from each other. Lil said I was a gypsy, moving with Al. I didn't hear from my brother often so I was shocked to get a phone call from Dan, who was married and Living in Ogdensburg again. He said our father had a heart attack and passed away suddenly on April 29th, 1949. He had closed his store and gone home to his apartment at the end of the day, not feeling well. Dan said they would wait to hear from us before making any funeral arrangements. We couldn't afford it but we borrowed $1,000.00 from our neighbors and arranged to fly to New York. Al and Ricky stayed with his parents in Brooklyn and I took the train from New York city to Ogdensburg. My brother met me at the train station and drove me directly to the funeral parlor. They were holding up the funeral until my arrival. My stepmother did not even say hello to me. My father's older brother, my uncle Sam, had died in Maine on April 19th, but my pop did not find out about it until April 29th and he was so upset that he started having chest pains. He was all alone because his wife, my stepmother, was away in Montreal visiting her sister. When he got home after closing his store he knocked on the door next door and and asked for help. His neighbor, who was a fireman, drove him to the hospital, where he passed away.

Lillian and Jim and several other people attended the funeral, but I don't remember anything about it. My Stepmother ignored me as if I wasn't even there. The whole thing was a blur. After the burial, we went to Jim's parents' house. His mom, Mrs. Williams, made tuna sandwiches and I realized I hadn't eaten and was very hungry. That's where I saw my twin nephews, Bobby and Johnny, for the first time. They were sitting in highchairs in the kitchen and their grandma Williams was feeding them lunch. They were around sixteen months old and as cute as could be. I went back to Alexandria Bay with Lil and the following day took the train back to New York, where Al and Ricky were waiting for me at his parents' house in Brooklyn. We stayed there for a week before flying back to California. Ricky was nine months old and was adorable. Al's parents begged us to stay and not return to L.A. Al only had a short time left before he graduated from West Coast University and had to finish, so we had to go back. His parents gave him the money we needed to pay back our neighbors.

CHAPTER **22**

AFTER AL GRADUATED, he started job-hunting. He put in applications with all the airlines but nobody would hire him without experience. His parents talked him into returning to NY, so we packed up again and left California. We stayed with Al's parents until we could get settled. His father had a lot of relatives and everyday he made plans for Al to take him visiting and show off his precious grandson, Ricky. When Al did go job hunting he didn't have any luck. I got discouraged and took Ricky and went by bus to northern NY to see Lil and her family. I was there about a week when Al showed up. He couldn't stand it without me, so he bought a cheap old car, fixed it, and drove to A-bay.

Lil got the Syracuse newspaper every day. Al saw an ad under business opportunities for someone to manage a Shell gas station in Syracuse. Al knew the Shell supervisor who placed the ad. He was the same man who was the Shell supervisor before the war when Al had a Shell station in Brooklyn. We went to Syracuse and Al took over the gas station. We found an apartment a block away. We lived there for around a year when I saw an ad in the help wanted section of the newspaper for an Airline looking for instrument repair technicians for Robinson airlines in Ithaca, NY. I sent for an application and without Al's knowledge I applied for the job for him. When they replied, and said they were interested, I confessed and told him to make arrangements for one of his employees to run the station so he could get away and go to Ithaca for the interview. He was hired, and had to find a qualified person to take over the gas station. Once again, we had to move from Syracuse to Ithaca. Al went first to find an apartment. He was really excited about finally having a job in aviation.

CHAPTER **23**

MARGARET WAS STILL in Ithaca. She was happy to hear we were moving back. She helped Al find an apartment. Al had to set up the whole electronics department. He built the work benches, purchased the necessary equipment and made use of all the knowledge he gained from West Coast University. Robinson airlines only had five planes to start with. Before Al was hired they had to use an outside company to maintain the instruments. They planned to grow, added new routes and purchased more planes and expanded rapidly. They changed the company name to Mohawk airlines. Al went to see Mr. Peters at the old flying school. He was so glad to hear that Al took his advice and went to West Coast University and now had a job repairing aircraft instruments.

I was pregnant again and Ricky was almost three. Around my due date Al drove to NY and brought his parents to Ithaca to take care of Ricky when I had the new baby. On my due date, I woke up not feeling too great. His mom suggested I take Al's dad and sit outside on the front porch for a while on one of the rocking chairs for fresh air. I started having labor pains and Al's mom asked me not to tell his dad, who had Parkinson's disease or he would get too nervous and shake more than ever. I went out on the front porch to sit with him but the pains were getting stronger. I knew I couldn't wait for Al to come home from work so I snuck inside and called a taxi. By then the labor pains were so strong I barely made it to the hospital. When I paid the taxi driver he was so afraid he might have to deliver the baby that he dropped the change and I told him to keep it. I delivered the baby the minute I arrived. The doctor wasn't even there yet. Meanwhile grandpa Friedland was still sitting on the front porch rocking, wondering where I was.

Al came home from work and his dad was cussing me out he was mad at me for leaving him alone and disappearing. They could hardly believe that I had gone to the hospital alone by cab. Al looked in the closet and under the bed, thinking I was playing tricks on him. We named our new baby Philip. When I brought him home from the hospital, Ricky, who was almost three, took one look at him and said, "that's enough." He said we didn't need a baby around. He said we should send him back or throw him in the garbage. We put Philip in the crib and he turned over at five days old. Grandma said he is a Flipper because he flipped over. We have been calling him Flipper ever Since. Grandma called him slipper but meant Flipper.

CHAPTER **24**

ROBINSON AIRLINES GREW and changed the company name to Mohawk airlines. As soon as we were confident that Al's job was stable, we went house hunting. We found a nice piece of property within our budget on Stone Quarry Road. It was on a hill opposite the hill where Cornell University was located. It was right next to Upper Buttermilk State Park, which was the boundary of our property and overlooked Cayuga lake. There was a very nice well maintained ranch type three-bedroom house in front and a small one bedroom furnished cottage in back. We rented the cottage to a female Cornell University professor. She rented it annually but traveled during the summer when college was out. She said we could use it while she was gone if we fed her two outside cats and she could leave her belongings there. This was perfect for us because Al's parents could spend summers in Ithaca with us and have their own place. The rent paid the mortgage.

In the fall, when college started. The professor returned and Al drove his parents back home to NY. Grandpa said he felt like a king listening to the chimes peal from Cornell up on the hill where we lived. Grandma did most of the cooking in our big house. My aunt Hannah came to visit, too. When they were Both there at the same time they shared the cooking. We never ate out! I learned a lot by watching them. They both knew how to bake strudel, but each was different. They squabbled over which was better. Now, when I bake strudel I make a combination of both. They were both excellent cooks. Delicious stuff!!! We did not have trash pick up where we lived. Al had to take it to the dump. We still had the Pekingese dog, Chinky who was adorable. She loved to ride in the car on the ledge over the back seat and look out the rear window. As soon as the car door opened she would jump in. Al was busy with the trash and didn't notice her. After a while the kids asked where Chinky was. We called her and looked all over, but she was nowhere to be found. Al came home from the dump without her. Then, I remembered that the last time I saw her was before al went to the dump. We all jumped in the car and went back there. She was sitting on a pile of garbage waiting patiently for us.

They had an agricultural college at Cornell where they taught the latest scientific methods for raising cattle and farming. There was a retail outlet store on the premises where they sold the products. We bought the freshest meat, eggs, dairy products, fruit and vegetables for less than supermarket prices. Once a week we went there and shopped. Grandma Friedland said the chickens were college educated because they each knew which nest was theirs to lay their eggs in. Everyone knows that you can buy good food in New York city, but when they went back to Brooklyn they loaded up with stuff from Cornell in a large cooler before leaving at summer's end. While we were living in Ithaca I decided to learn to drive. The football coach at Cornell taught adult drivers ed. classes at night at Ithaca high school during spring off-season. I had to practice between lessons. On a Saturday afternoon, Al took me out to practice on a country road. He told me to back up. I looked in the rear-view mirror and saw Flipper in the back seat hanging out of the car window. One leg was in the car and the rest of him was ready to fall out. I hollered for him to get back in the car and backed up into a muddy ditch. We could not get the car out of the ditch. Al walked to the nearest farm house and borrowed some wood so he could get enough traction to get us out. Then he drove us home. He called me a big dummy and said I would never pass the driving test. I practiced some more and one of my friends picked me up and drove me downtown to take the driving test. I passed the first time.

The airlines sent Al to California representing them

to inspect some Convair airplanes that the Flying Tiger Airlines were selling and make a bid on them. While he was gone, Ricky got the mumps, it was a cold winter with lots of ice and snow. The garage sliding door froze shut and I couldn't get the car out of the garage. Ricky wrote his dad a letter and said you must come home because I have the mumps and mommy can't get the car out of the garage.

CHAPTER **25**

FLIPPER STARTED KINDERGARTEN when he was five and Al got me a part-time job as a clerk with Mohawk airlines credit union. I would walk Ricky and Flipper to school and take the bus to the credit union. I worked mornings until it was time to pick Flipper up from his half-day in kindergarten. Due to the harsh winter weather, Al kept getting bad respiratory infections. After a couple of bouts with Pneumonia his doctor said he had to move to a warmer climate. So, the gypsies, as Lil called us, sold our property in Ithaca and headed south to Florida. I was pregnant with my third child. Al left the boys and me in Brooklyn with his parents. His sister went with him from Brooklyn to Florida. He drove our car pulling a UHaul trailer with as much as we could load into it. He found a motel on Biscayne Blvd. in Miami for us to stay in until we could find an apartment to rent. His sister flew home and I flew to Miami with Ricky and Flipper. Al picked us up at the airport and took us to the motel temporarily. He was working for the instrument dept. of Eastern Airlines and the Florida weather was wonderful after Ithaca.

While we were staying at the motel we met another family who were relocating from Long Island, NY to Florida. They had four nice young boys who played with our two sons. The wife was very sweet. It was the middle of April and my baby was due the middle of June. She asked me who was going to take care of my Two kids and our Pekingese dog when I went to the hospital to have the new baby. I told her I would have to find someone and she offered to do it. She said her husband was gone a lot on business and it would not be a problem. So, we kept in touch. We rented an apartment in a new duplex in Miami. They rented an apartment in Coral Gables. We talked on the phone every day. They were Italian and she cooked big pots of spaghetti and invited us over a couple of times a week. When I started having labor pains, she told us to come over because her place was closer to Mercy Hospital than ours was. When the pains got closer, Al left the kids there and took me to the hospital where my doctor was waiting. I had the baby quickly and Al went home to call his family and tell them we had another boy.

CHAPTER 26

WHEN AL CALLED his parents, he was told that his father had just passed away and he needed to fly to NY immediately. He changed his clothes, packed a few things, and went to the airport to take the next flight to NY. He showed his Eastern Airlines Id and flew to NY without a ticket. He didn't have time to call anyone and tell us he was going. After the funeral, he called our friend in Coral Gables who was taking care of the kids. She could find a neighbor to watch them while she took a taxi to the hospital to tell me what happened. I was so relieved to hear that Al hadn't just deserted me. While I was in the hospital a nurse asked me to fill out the papers with the baby's name. We had not discussed names because we didn't even know the gender. By then I knew I had to choose a name after Al's father for the birth certificate. I didn't want Jacob or Jake so decided on Jay. They said I needed a middle name and suggested "Lee" (after general Lee). I was told that Jay would be a special person because he had a name waiting for him when he was born in June of 1957. That's how my third son was named Jay Lee.

After five days, they discharged me from the hospital. I had no money for a taxi so I called my new neighbor, Jane who lived in the other duplex apartment next to ours. She sent her husband to pick me up. When I walked into our apartment alone carrying my new son, Jay, I found a mess. Al was in such a rush to go to NY that he left the windows open and it had rained in. There were puddles on the floor. He had changed clothes and the old ones were in a pile. The new crib was still in the cardboard box against the wall waiting to be put together. They had given me baby formula at the hospital but the new baby bottles had not been sterilized. I put the baby down in the middle of our big bed and cried. Just then the phone rang. It was Al's aunt calling from NY to tell me Al would fly home after sundown. My neighbors came in and the husband put the crib together and the wife sterilized the bottles and divided the formula in them. I had washed the new crib sheets. I made the crib, warmed a bottle of formula, fed Jay, and he went to sleep in the crib. I picked up Al's dirty clothes. When I put them in the clothes hamper I found that Al had thrown his shoes in there instead of the dirty clothes. I mopped the puddles up. By then I was exhausted, so both the baby and I slept.

CHAPTER **27**

 AL FLEW HOME that night. He stopped to pick up the kids and our dog on the way home. He thanked our friend and tried to pay her but she refused his money. He told her we would be back to show her the baby the following weekend. On the way home Ricky told Al a shocking story about what happened. He said one evening while they were there a man was banging on the door saying to open the door or he would break it down. He said he was from the FBI. The kids were told to run and hide under the beds or in the closet in case there were gunshots. The husband was with the mafia, which we didn't know, and was wanted on a murder charge. The FBI agents left after they saw only a woman, kids, and our dog. The husband had left and gone to NY and never came back after he moved his wife and kids into that Coral Gables apartment, we didn't suspect anything. Al told her we would be back with our new baby, Jay.

The following weekend Al bought a box of chocolates and a bouquet of flowers and we went to thank her for taking care of Ricky and Flipper. There was a "for rent" sign on the window and the apartment was empty. I was horrified to think we could have lost our children. We never saw or heard from them again. Al had brought his mother back with him on the plane to stay with us for a while in Florida. She never flew before and was scared and sat all huddled in her seat. When they landed she said she could have enjoyed it. Now she saw why Al loved flying so much and never thought she would be one of the "crazy ones" flying. Since she had never been to Florida before she marveled at how beautiful it was with palm trees and flowers. She said she never realized how much sky there was. She loved playing with her grandchildren and going to Miami beach. New York has many sights, but nothing like the south beach hotels and all the open spaces.

After dinner, we sat on the front porch and when she smelled the night blooming jasmine she said it was a magical land where there was perfume in the air. We went grocery shopping and she bought the ingredients for one of Al's favorite dishes, a carrot tzimmes stew. I was getting ready to wash the baby clothes and prepared a cup of ivory snow for the laundry. She thought I poured a cup of sugar for her cooking and put it in the pot with the meat, chicken, carrots and sweet potatoes. After I gathered the diapers and other baby clothes I asked her where the soap was and she said she didn't realize it was soap. She thought it was sugar and had put it in the pot with the other ingredients. By that time, it was bubbling and making suds. I told her we couldn't eat it and had to throw the whole thing out. She said she would fix it and started washing the bubbles out of the pot of food. She washed and washed it and said now it was ok. I said I wouldn't eat any and wouldn't let Ricky or Flipper eat any. When Al came home from work he asked what's cooking. He said he was starved and something smelled great. She served him a very small portion. He asked why she only gave him such a little bit. I started laughing hysterically and finally told him the truth. Talk about too many cooks spoiling the broth!!! Needless to say, we ate something else that night. At the end of August when the kids went back to school Al took grandma back to Brooklyn by plane. When our lease ran out we decided to buy a house instead of renting. Most of the eastern airlines employees Al worked with lived in Hialeah because it was close to the airport and like a small town.

CHAPTER **28**

WE BOUGHT A nice corner house in a quiet neighborhood close to schools. We had the only house with sidewalks and Jay was allowed to ride his tricycle to the end of the sidewalk both ways. I could watch him out of the windows and he only went to the end of the sidewalk. He wore a little hat with a red feather sticking up so I could see him. In May of 1961 I was pregnant again. I was hoping for A daughter and was going to name her after my grandmother, Sara Lee Katz, whom I had never met. Al didn't want another child, but I wanted a girl.

Lisa Sue was born a few minutes after midnight on February 1st. I saw her immediately after she was born and was so excited to finally have a girl that I stayed up all night. I was afraid that if I fell asleep they would tell me I had another boy. Grandma Sadie flew down again to take care of the three boys. She was a very colicky baby. She didn't just cry but screamed in pain constantly. Al called our cousin in Maryland and she came to help us take care of Lisa but she couldn't make her stop. When Lisa was just six weeks old I had to have an operation. Lisa cried so much that the doctor said she needed testing and She had to be hospitalized, too. They brought a crib into my room. When she cried, I rang for the nurse and the nurse fed and changed her she still had colic. We were both discharged together. She cried until she was about a year old. After a while it became a bad habit. She cried until she could talk. I made Her promise she wouldn't cry and that's when she Finally stopped. Lisa was a very beautiful little Girl with dimples and big green eyes and lots of dark Hair. Once when Al was carrying her out of a department store he was stopped by a security guard who thought he had shoplifted a doll.

CHAPTER **29**

WE BECAME GOOD friends with an elderly Spanish couple who babysat for us. When Jay started first grade and Rick and Flipper were in school we were thinking about how we could afford to send the boys to college. Although Al made a good salary we knew I would have to go back to work. I answered an ad in the paper for an experienced credit union clerk. I was called in for an interview. It happened that Tita, our nanny, was available to take care of Lisa and Jay and there was no school that day. Ricky was playing ball in the street when I was leaving. He asked me where I thought I was going all dressed up in a pretty dress, wearing high heels and lipstick. When I told him I saw an ad and was going for a job. He started laughing so hard he was rolling around in the street. He said nobody would hire me, I was just a mom and didn't know how to do office work. The person who was interviewing me at the credit union was an eighteen-year-old girl. She told me I was too old at age thirty-six for the job. So, I went back home Ricky said he told me I wouldn't get the job.

A few days later I got a call from a lady who asked me to come to her office. It was in the main office building of the parent company of the credit union. She was secretary of the board of directors. She said she had looked over the applications and resumes that had been submitted. She liked mine best. She said I was the only one who had any credit union experience previously and a good letter of reference. I was the most qualified. She wondered why the girl who interviewed me didn't hire me. Then I said the only reason she gave me was that at 36 I was too old. She laughed and said she was a year older than I was. I was hired and ready to start. There were no age discrimination laws back then. She told me to go back to the credit union office the following Monday ready to start working. Ricky couldn't believe I got the job. I decided for our Tita and Pedro to take care of Lisa and for Jay to go there after school. I started working full time the beginning of December 1963.

CHAPTER **30**

THE FIRST DAY on my new job the eighteen-year-old girl who was my boss asked me if I knew how to figure dividends on the savings accounts. I said I did and she brought me a big pile to start on. I asked for a calculator and the interest rate and started computing them with the factor I needed. She was shocked and brought me another stack to work on. She started to like me because I knew how to do the work and made her job easier. I knew more than the other two girls who worked there. One posted payments to the accounts and the other one mainly answered the phone. I learned that the reason they hired another person was because the manager died unexpectedly. The board of directors appointed the young girl who was working there as a clerk to temporary manager until they could find a more qualified manager. She was the one who thought I was too old! The secretary of the board of directors placed an ad in the national credit union magazine looking for an experienced credit union manager. They chose a man who was an automobile dealer finance manager. He was very nice and intelligent, but had no credit union experience. The first day he came in the office the girl who thought I was too old to hire and was temporary manager quit and walked out of the office. I continued doing most of the work and taught him a lot. He stayed a few months and after he learned enough he gave notice that he was leaving to go to work as manager of the city of Miami beach credit union.

That left our office with no manager again. By now I was doing everything, including all the monthly financial reports and working with the Federal auditors. The president of the board of directors came to the office and asked me if there was someplace I could go with him where we could talk confidentially. The only place in the office was a closet where we stored our membership cards, loan applications, envelopes, blank checks and records. We entered, turned on the light, shut the door, and he started talking. He offered me the job as credit union manager with a large raise in salary. I hesitated because as I told him I had four kids and a sick husband. He knew I was too conscientious to take time off unless it was absolutely necessary. He told me I was doing all the work anyway, so I might as well take the title and the raise. I wanted to talk to Al first. We thought about it and said I would try it on a temporary basis for ninety days. If the board was satisfied with the job I was doing and if I didn't have any problems at home it would then become permanent. We shook hands and were going to come out of the closet and tell the girls what we decided. But we discovered that the closet door didn't have a handle inside and there was no way we could open it. We started banging on the door and inside walls but nobody heard us Because the old N.C.R. posting machine used for payroll deduction payments was so loud and noisy. Finally, I got a phone call and one of the girls knocked on the door and let us out. My new boss said he never thought it would be so hard to get someone to take a promotion and raise.

CHAPTER 31

DURING THE 30 years, I worked at the credit union there was never a dull moment. I attended credit union management meetings with the other area credit union managers and learned a lot that helped our members with financial counseling, meeting their needs. I listened to their problems and tried to help them. Some of our members were illiterate and required help completing the loan applications. Among the questions was sex. One person checked it and said "yes, and lots of it". I was conscientious doing a good job and putting extra effort in so things would run smoothly. I reread the loan applications and ran credit checks before presenting them to the credit committee. I made sure that everything balanced. I sent reminder notices to the directors of the board meetings together with all pertinent information.

Computers were coming in and we converted to a system devised especially for credit unions. The members were treated like people and not a number. Even after we went on computers. At the time of the conversion another employee and I had to go to a bank in downtown Miami that ran the system. We only had monitors in our office and had to be trained on them. We got home at 2 a.m. the night of the conversion. Al was not happy that night. Because I was a notary public I could perform marriages. One couple asked me if they could come to my home for me to perform the ceremony. On the way home from the office I stopped and bought a bottle of wine and a cake. When I got home the couple had arrived before me with the bride's mother and kid brother. The kid was chubby and had split the crotch of his pants. Needless to say, I had a hard time reading the wedding words from the notary booklet without bursting out laughing. Afterwards we had a wine toast and the cake. When they left, I sat down with my hubby and kids and we had dinner. My kids said none of their friends' moms were like me. They told me I had a weird job.

One of my duties was to get new members to join our credit union. I had to go to the parent company supermarkets at various locations from Key West to west Palm Beach. I talked to the employees and bragged About the benefits of membership with payroll deduction of as little as a $1.00 a week, they could start saving without noticing until their quarterly statements arrived. I reported at the monthly board of directors' meetings how many new accounts I signed. We paid higher interest on savings and charged lower interest on loans. We also did financial counseling. Because of my position, I was given a rental car and free gas. I had to fill up where the company trucks got their gas. One day the attendant at the gas pump asked me if I would marry him. I told him I already had a husband. He said he meant he wanted me to marry him to his girlfriend. I asked him if they had a marriage license and he said they would get one. A couple of days later they showed up at the credit union office in the morning in his truck. She was barefoot. I asked if she had a bouquet and she said she had left It in the truck. She ran out in her bare feet to get it. They came into my office and two of the girls in the office were the witnesses. Afterwards, we laughed hysterically. A few months later the groom came to my office and said they were getting divorced. I told him to think it over, because they would spoil my good record of around twenty happy marriages I performed. He told me that he had gone to work one morning but didn't feel well so he turned around and went home and found his wife in bed with another man, that's why he was filing for divorce.

I was also responsible for making sure we received the loan payments on time and had to work on collecting the overdue payments. Some of the car loans became delinquent and after exhausting all means of collecting them it was necessary to call a repossession company. I hesitated to do it and only got the courage by remembering that I had my own payments to make and these losers were no better than I was. One of the cars we repo'd belonged to the nephew of a mafia big shot and they threatened to get even. The cars were stored in the company warehouse fenced-in lot. A few were paid off and reclaimed but most were resold to the highest bidder. I told the borrower his mafia uncle could pay. Another repo car had stolen meat hidden in the trunk and it started to smell awful. Apparently, the owner of the car planned to take home the meat but we repossessed it meat and all. Another one had a whole trunk full of cases of tuna fish. When he saw his car inside the yard with the other repos he climbed over the fence, opened the trunk, and started throwing cases of tuna fish over the fence. He got caught! They started calling me "used car Sam". I hated it. At the end of every day we balanced everything and prepared the bank deposit which I dropped off at the drive-thru window on the way home. One day as I was doing this the teller said that the deposit didn't add up. She called the security guard and I was afraid I was going to jail. I asked her to just give it back to me and I left. When I got home I checked it and found some of the cash had been removed and a personal check was put in to replace it, but the deposit slip was not corrected. The following day when the girls came to work I was very angry and swore and said I never wanted to see them do anything sneaky like that again. The girl who was the culprit took down the big wall calendar and wrote on it "Estelle swore today" I could write a whole book on my credit union years!!! I worked there for 30 years and didn't know what I would do when I retired. I had a nice retirement party.

CHAPTER **32**

I FOUND PLENTY to do. My friends, Jeannie, Jane and I started traveling. Sometimes Jane's daughter, Heidi, came with us. We went on 32 cruises everywhere. We had many wonderful experiences. When Heidi came with us we hired taxicabs rather than going on the bus tours arranged by the ship. In Turkey, the handsome taxi driver took us sightseeing first and then to his parents' home in Istanbul to meet his family. His father grew fig trees, dried and packaged the figs and sold them at the grand bazaar in Istanbul. He was married to a beautiful English girl who he met while she was on a vacation camping trip with some girlfriends in Turkey. She was pregnant and was very happy to have Americans visit them. She was learning Turkish. She said at first when he proposed she refused. But when she went back to England she realized she loved him. She returned and everyone in the area attended their huge Christian wedding. While we were talking, the mother baked us fresh pastries filled with figs. They were delicious. We bought some pack-aged figs to take home. He took me to a small local jewelry store where the owners wife made a pair of earrings for my Lisa. We gave our taxi driver a gener-ous tip when he drove us back to the ship. We had an unforgettable time.

When we went to Greece we found an English-speaking taxi driver to take us sightseeing. We told him about our wonderful experience in turkey. Not to be outdone, he offered to take us to meet his parents. His father had been a city bus driver in Athens. After he retired they bought a home in the mountains where they grew olive trees and planted a huge garden. He tried to call his mother on his cellphone to tell her he was bringing guests home. When she didn't answer, he said she must be working outside in her garden. He opened the car window and stuck his head out and shouted "mama", "mama" and it echoed all through the mountains. He said now she would know we were coming. She welcomed us and made us lunch. She picked fresh spinach and tomatoes from her gar-den. She made a dough and rolled it out and mixed spices and olive oil in the spinach she stuffed it in the dough in individual pockets. While she was baking that she made a salad of her own pickled olives and fresh tomatoes and herbs. Yes, the food on the cruise ship was good, it didn't compare with the gourmet inexpensive meal she made. She offered us wine from the grapevines her husband grew. We thanked her and tried to pay her but she refused. So, of course we tipped the driver generously when he drove us back to our ship.

How many American tourists are as fortunate as we were? We went to many other memorable places on cruises including the pyramids in Egypt. Jeannie and Jane rode camels there. We were warned the camels might gallop away and the Arabs would hold the brave riders for ransom. Arabs tried to put their red and white head coverings on us. I said, "no way". They were dirty and smelly and probably full of bugs. When we get together we reminisce about our trips. We also went on a Mississippi paddlewheel boat river cruise. We thought we were lucky to have a cabin with three beds and a balcony with French doors right over the paddle wheel. When we went to the dining room for dinner we left the French doors open. While we were away the paddleboat started moving Jane's bed was just inside the open French doors. The paddle wheel splashed water in and her bed was soaking wet. We couldn't find anyone to help us. Jane went out in the hall where she found a linen cart with dry sheets, pillows, and blankets and remade her bed. We never left the French doors open again. On that trip, we visited antebellum houses and historic sites. We went to a store in Baton Rouge where they had millions of buttons. We did all kinds of unusual things. We had the wanderlust and went on exciting odysseys. We went to San Francisco and saw the sights and rode on an open trolley car. We rented a car and took turns driving through snow in the Sierra Madre mountains. We got behind a snow plow that threw snow on the car and drove to Reno and then on to Las Vegas.

We belonged to the Broward theatre for performing arts and saw all the Broadway shows. We also went to all the amateur Pembroke Pines shows. Our friend, Eddie, Jeannie and I had season tickets to shows in a Miami beach hotel. After the shows, we took turns going to each other's houses for dinner. When I wasn't traveling or busy doing other things I had time to visit and help my old disabled friend, Clara, who was legally blind and lived in Boca Raton. I took her to lunch, grocery shopping, and wherever she needed to go. She had a very wealthy sister, Ella, whom we would visit in Palm Beach at her mansion. Ella arranged a special 70th birthday party for me at the exclusive governors' club of the Palm Beaches. Although she had a chauffeur, she drove us there in her Rolls Royce. We had a gourmet banquet birthday lunch. She gave me a beautiful, expensive Cartier clock as a 70th birthday gift. Ella and her husband, Sam, a famous retired plastic surgeon, wanted to show me how much they appreciated everything I did for poor Clara. We visited them quite often.

CHAPTER **33**

ON THE FIRST day, I went to work in 1963 when Lisa was a year old, I took Jay to school, as usual, and I told him to call me when he got home after school. He told me it was raining and he got all wet walking home and I didn't even care. Before, I would walk him to school with an umbrella on rainy days. Then, I would pick him up and walk him home after. I told him I did care but I didn't have any windows in my office and didn't even know it was raining. He put a guilt trip on me, one of many. With both parents working, the boys had chores to do. The beds all had to be made, dishes done, and no messes left around. I took Lisa to her nanny's and drove the boys to school on my way to work. Al got home around the same time the boys got home from school.

Sometimes I left notes on the refrigerator door telling them what to start preparing for dinner. We had a great Italian restaurant nearby and Rick would go there with a large pot which they would fill with the best spaghetti and meatballs for $4.00. Once when Rick went there he witnessed a driver of another vehicle hit the restaurant owners parked car and leave. He told the people in the restaurant who called the police and Rick became the hero. After that they always gave us full pots. I didn't find out until years later that Ricky and Flipper talked Jay into making their beds for them. They told him he was in training to become a hotel manager. He loved staying in hotels whenever we went on vacation. He also loved the Ed Sullivan show on TV. They would play the Nutcracker Suite on the stereo and make him toe dance around the living room, saying if he got good enough he could be on Ed Sullivan's show.

I wanted Lisa to stay with her nanny until I got home, but sometimes the boys would go and get her and bring her home. When they terrorized her, she climbed one of the two huge trees next to our house and hollered "I'm telling". They called her "the queen of the monkeys." They were mischievous but good kids. Ricky graduated from Hialeah high school and won a scholarship to the University of Miami. He didn't like it there and transferred to Florida State University in Tallahassee, where he graduated from college and law school. He passed the bar and became an attorney. Flipper went to Florida State, too, after visiting Ricky there. He graduated from Hialeah high school and lived in a dormitory the first year at FSU, after which he shared an apartment with Ricky. He became a CPA. The Cubans who escaped Castro started moving to Hialeah. When there was only one other American family left on our block we put our house up for sale. After Jay finished his sophomore year at Hialeah High School we bought a house in North Miami Beach and moved. Jay was so angry that he wouldn't talk to me all that summer. He did not want to move and leave his friends and change schools. He would ride his bike back to Hialeah to be with his friends or ride to the beach and spend the day there and be home for dinner.

CHAPTER 34

WHEN SCHOOL STARTED in September he transferred at the end of the summer. He went to North
Miami Beach senior high. That was the best thing that
could have happened. He made new friends and there
were better courses offered. He spent a lot of time in
the new modern lab and that's what influenced him to
study medicine. He and his good friend, Bob Singer,
bought guitars and spent hours on our back patio
playing and singing. He took a lot of college level
courses and "clepped out" of many classes when he
graduated and went to Florida State University. While
Jay was at FSU he tutored the football players in biol-
ogy and chemistry so they could keep their grades up
to be eligible to be on the team. He was paid by the
NCAA. The guys on the team called him "doc".

He did research with Dr. Hofer in the lab hoping
to find a cure for cancer. He got his bachelor's' degree
and his masters, writing a thesis on his experiments.

He used mice for his lab work. He found that they had mice in England with a different strain of cancer. He arranged to have mice from the Royal British Science Bank shipped to the Miami airport. I was working in my credit union office the day the mice were due to arrive. Jay called me at my office. He asked me to go to the cargo section at the airport and claim the mice coming in on a B.O.A. flight and take them to an Eastern Airline plane that was going to Tallahassee. Ricky had taken care of the necessary Customs clearance and everything was set. However, the B.O.A. flight arrived late and the last flight to Tallahassee had already taken off. The cargo employees said the next flight was at six a.m. the following morning. They would not be responsible for the mice overnight. I had to go home with them. They were in a large wooden crate with a screen over the top. When I walked in the house Al asked what I was carrying. I told him and he said I wasn't going to bring mice sick with cancer into our house. So, I took them out on the back patio. The next morning, I got up at five a.m. and shipped them off on eastern to Tallahassee. I called Jay and told him when they would arrive. Rather than go home, I went to my office early.

Jay said if he won the Nobel prize I would be very proud of him. Jay enrolled in the pims program, the FSU program in medical sciences, which was his first year in medical school. Since FSU did not have a med

95

school yet he had to go to the University of Florida Shands teaching hospital in Gainesville and leave Tallahassee. The students at U of Fla. (gators) were Seminole enemies. They saw Seminole stickers on his car and threw eggs and rotten tomatoes at it. During the summer when Jay came home from Tallahassee I was able to get a job for him with the dairy and deli department in the Skylake pantry pride supermarket. Al, Lisa, and I left Jay and Flip home and went up north on vacation. Jay was using my Chevy Impala to go to work and when he left work at the end of one day the car was not in the parking lot. He called Flip and told him to stop playing tricks on him and tell him where he moved the car to. Flip said he just got home from his job himself and didn't touch the car. Flip told him to call the police. The car had been stolen from the parking lot. After we came home from our trip Lisa's girlfriend came over and told us she saw our car in the bushes near her grandma's condo. She knew it was ours because it had FSU Seminole stickers on it. It had been hot wired and was ruined. We sold it to a girl who was going to fix it and use it to race in the "powder puff derby". She got under it on the ground and fixed the brakes and took off like a bat out of hell. I wrote to Jay who had left for college and he said he and his friends all laughed and laughed. Jay met Laura at FSU and they started dating. She was studying to be a nurse. They were married in a simple wedding in Tallahassee at Maclellan gardens on March 27, 1982.

Lisa and I drove up there to the wedding with her boyfriend P.J. in the Chevy Chevette I had given to Lisa as a high school graduation gift. She never liked it and had purchased a new Pontiac. Jay and Laura were thankful for the Chevy we left them as a gift. We flew back to Miami.

CHAPTER **35**

MAYBE IT WAS because of World War II or the pneumonia he suffered from in cold Ithaca, but Al did not have good health. His kidneys were not operating properly, he had nephritis, which was probably from using Varsol and other harsh chemicals for so many years to clean the instruments while he worked for the airlines. He also had kidney stones and the gout and was in a lot of pain. He had diabetes and hypertension, and then he developed a brain tumor on top of everything else. He had three major brain surgeries in one year. He called his head the onion head because of all the surgeries. He told me he didn't want any viewing or big funeral. He passed away on December 28, 1981.

He had said he didn't need a parade viewing his chopped-up head. We had a simple graveside service at Lakeside memorial gardens attended by family and friends. They closed the credit union for Al's funeral.

During that time, he was so ill and getting treated, Connie and Flip were making wedding plans and so were Jay and Laura. Previously, he was able to attend Rick's wedding to Joanne in Treasure Island in September of 1973. He was fine back then and did a lot of dancing. In fact, they called him twinkle toes. One of the last things Al said was he wanted to go to the other weddings. My brother, Dan, who had been in a nursing home after having a stroke, also passed away on a December 28th twenty-one years later in 2002. Dan had made prior arrangements to have his remains donated to the health center at Syracuse University upstate medical center for scientific research. His wife had predeceased him and they never had children. December 28th is a sad day for me. Both my husband and my brother passed away then.

I told Flip not to postpone his wedding to Connie which was planned for January 2nd, 1982. It was only a small wedding in Connie's parents' home in Pennsylvania and they did not have music. Only Connie's family attended. Connie is the best!!! Flip could not have chosen a more wonderful, lovelier wife. After they returned from Pennsylvania to Florida, friends Marion and Art arranged a beautiful belated wedding reception for them. I was devastated when Al passed away. He was my soulmate and the love of my life. I had boyfriends in high school and was dating a college guy who was studying to be a pharmacist when I met Al. Both came to see me at the same time at the girls' club. But I only had eyes for Al and everyone knew it. We had the kind of story-book love they make into movies. I would never consider remarrying. Nobody could ever take his place.

Lisa was not quite twenty years old and was then and always has been my "crutch". After she graduated from high school she had a job working for Jefferson's department store. She woke up one morning with bell's palsy. Our doctor sent her to Parkway hospital where she had daily therapy. While she was there, she found a job opening for a pharmacy technician and applied for it and got it. She also attended Broward community college. At the same time. She had to work different shifts on her job, including evenings and weekends. Part of her job was to deliver the meds to the different nurses' stations and while she was doing that one of the doctors approached her and offered her a job in his office. She told him she didn't have any experience in that. He told her he would train her. He was an excellent ear, nose, and throat specialist and she learned a lot from him. She worked in his office until he sold his practice and moved away. After that, an infectious disease specialist who was just starting his practice hired her and she has been with that office ever since. It's been over thirty-two years now.

CHAPTER **36**

AS I MENTIONED before, I don't know what I would do without Lisa. She always had a lot of girlfriends and boyfriends. When she was in high school she had a date with a kid to go to the movies and he stood her up. She was crying and upset so I told her I wanted to see that movie and we went and enjoyed it. Needless to say, she never saw that loser again. She stopped seeing another guy because he was "smothering" her. And then there was that cop. After they went out one night and he drank too much. He brought her home late. I was already asleep and didn't hear them. I didn't know if he was in one of our spare rooms, on the couch, or in bed with Lisa, but he got up during the night to go to the bathroom and mistakenly got in bed in my room with me. I woke up and when I realized what happened I kicked him out and startled giggling and laughed all night. In the morning, he left before I got up. They fought quite a lot. He always managed to get nice birthday and

Christmas presents from her but never reciprocated. They finally broke up.

Her friend, Paulette, one of the girls she worked with, and her new husband bought a nice new house and invited us to an art party she was having. The house next door to theirs was bought by a young guy who had four brothers. They were all invited to the party, too. Besides getting a free original art painting for hosting the party, it was a housewarming affair. They had a lot of friends, both girls and guys, and there was some matchmaking going on. The new neighbor, Randy, got Lisa's phone number and wanted to take me home and take her out. It was getting late and she had to work the next day so she refused. She started getting phone calls from him. She went out with Randy, Paulette's neighbor, and they started going steady. About three weeks later she came home Sunday night and told me he proposed to her and they were going to get married. I was shocked and said she didn't know him well enough, but she said he was the one. Although I had met his parents at the party I didn't know anything about them. The kids arranged for us to get together and when I saw that they were a good normal family I gave them my blessings. They made a beautiful couple.

CHAPTER **37**

I TOOK A day off from work at the credit union to go Looking with Lisa's future mother-in-law for a place to have the wedding. They belonged to a small yacht club and suggested holding it there, with the bride coming by boat. But Lisa wanted a traditional wedding gown with a long train which would be too cumbersome on their boat. We finally found a hall in Miramar and a D.J. and a catering company called "have your next affair with us" and a photographer and all the other things. We went shopping for a wedding gown and tuxedo shop. Then I asked our family friend, Art, who was an attorney and notary public if he would perform a simple ceremony and read some romantic poetry. Since Al had passed away, Lisa asked Rick, her oldest brother if he would give her away. He told her he had been trying to throw her away since she was born and would be honored to do it.

While Ramona and I were making arrangements,

we became good friends and our two families have been close ever since. The wedding turned out to be awesome. The catered buffet food was delicious, the hall was decorated beautifully, the D.J. made it a fun party. Everybody ate, drank, and danced. The photographer did a great job and we have the pictures to prove it. I paid for the wedding, gave them luggage to use on their honeymoon, and arranged a honeymoon package to Acapulco, Mexico which included airfare, a hotel and sightseeing. I did not expect Randy to get a kidney stone attack in the hotel in Mexico and ruin the whole honeymoon while he was in pain.

CHAPTER **38**

I PUT MY house up for sale now that Lisa was getting married and bought a condo. I had to get rid of a lot of stuff that accumulated over the years and pack up what I was going to move with me to my new condo. I asked the kids to come and take what they wanted, had a garage sale, gave away a lot, threw out what nobody wanted and left a large sectional sofa and China cabinet behind for the new owners. My sister who had come to Florida for the wedding helped me pack and get ready for the move. At first, she was dismayed to hear I was moving to a condominium. She pictured a big, tall skyscraper with an elevator. She was delighted when she saw my condo at Rolling Hills. It was on the ground floor and had a very large bedroom with twin beds, a nice kitchen, dining room, living room, screen-enclosed patio and was on a lake. The landscaping was so beautiful that the movie "Caddyshack" was made there on the golf course and country club.

Lil stayed with me and we had a good time until she went back to Alex Bay. Rolling Hills was close to my office. When I moved there the condo board asked me if I would join the board of directors and be the secretary treasurer of the condo association. Apparently, they had seen the required application form I had filled out for approval before I was allowed to move there. When they found out I was a credit union manager they asked me to take that position. I was really flattered. I took the minutes at the board meetings and followed "Robert's rules of order" (which they had never done before). I set up separate reserve accounts for the necessary expenses. I typed and distributed the board minutes. When the residents found out who I was, it became a nuisance. Every time they saw me they stopped me and told me their complaints, so I started dodging them. Being on a condo board is no fun!

When Lisa and Randy went to Acapulco on their honeymoon and Randy got the kidney stone attack he was in terrible pain. Lisa called the desk clerk and in Spanish told them. He arranged to get a doctor and some pain medication. They told Lisa it was too dangerous for her to go outside of the hotel by herself, so she had to stay with Randy in the hotel room while he suffered. She called home and told me but there was nothing I could do. Lil was still visiting me when they were scheduled to fly home and came with me to the airport. I had arranged for a wheelchair for Randy but thankfully he did not need it. The two of them came bouncing off the plane wearing straw hats and looking like nothing happened (after their honeymoon was ruined by his kidney stone attack).

CHAPTER **39**

WHEN LIL WENT home to Alexandria Bay it was quiet living alone, but I met some of the others who lived there. The president of the board of directors and his wife invited me to go out with them whenever they went out to dinner. I enjoyed my view of the lake. Everything was fine until my apartment was robbed. I went to work one morning around 7:30 a.m. when I returned home around 5:30 p.m. My front door was slightly ajar. I was sure I had locked it because I am a creature of habit. I entered it anyway and went into my bedroom. I found a disaster!

All the dresser drawers had been dumped out and the contents were thrown all over the room. The pillowcases were removed from the pillows on the bed. My jewelry was taken (probably thrown in the Pillow cases), my sterling silverware was gone from the china cabinet drawer, and my new V.C.R. player was no longer on the TV thankfully, everything was covered by my homeowners' insurance. My precious wedding ring was not replaceable and there was a limit of $1,000.00 on the other jewelry, I called the Davie police and within minutes they arrived. The officer said I never should have opened the door when I found it unlocked. The robbers would have killed me if they were still there. The cops made a mess looking for fingerprints and checking everything and gave me a police report and claim number. Not long after that someone broke my car window and stole my stereo system, speakers and all. I had a burglar alarm system installed in the apartment and in the car.

CHAPTER **40**

I WAS LIVING in my Rolling Hills condo and they were in their first house in Davie when Lisa got pregnant. I was working in my credit union when their first son, Jason, was born in June of 1986. Right after work. I rushed to the hospital. Lisa had to have a c section. It was on Ramona's birthday and he was her first grandchild. When Dr. Edelstein, Lisa's boss, came to the hospital to visit her, she was still under anesthesia, he told her she was flying without an airplane.

I can't begin to say what a great kid Jason has been. He is the one who named me Mommo. His other Mommo, Ramona, took care of him until he was old enough to start pre-school at sterling academy. I usually drove him to school in my car on my way to work at the credit union. Lisa and Randy bought a license plate for my car that said "Mommo's Taxi". During the time Jason was at sterling academy in a play and performing on stage dancing the Tarantella with a little girl, she fell off the stage and the music kept playing so he kept dancing alone. She wasn't hurt. He always did what was expected of him and more. After graduation from high school he enlisted in the Coast Guard where he served four years. He finished basic training in Cape May, N.J. and then the Coast Guard sent him to culinary school in Petaluma, California. His best friend, Nick, drove out with him. On the way, they stopped in Vegas to visit our good friend, Warren, and his mom.

He drove all alone home from Northern California to South Florida in 3 days.

Jason was assigned as a chef on a coast guard cutter. There was a crew of 104. He had to order enough food, prepare menus for three meals a day, cook and serve everyone. The ship chased and caught drug dealers and people on makeshift vessels and rafts throughout the Caribbean. After he had all kinds of experiences during those four years he went to college. When he graduated from Full Sail University with a bachelor's' degree in computer sciences. He started a website business first in Tallahassee. Now he lives in Atlanta, Ga. and worked as a U.I. software engineer for Turner Broadcasting. He left there for an even better position with Stanley Black & Decker in a new Digital division where every day there's a new challenge.

Jason met his spouse, Alan, while in college in Miami. They were married in Connecticut, and bought a beautiful home in a suburb of Atlanta. Alan is a wonderful bass baritone opera singer. Alan, too, calls me Mommo and they are very different but both successful in their careers. Our only regret is that they're so far away, but there are lots of phone calls and texts. We have a close relationship in spite of the distance.

CHAPTER 41

I AM SO LUCKY to have two sons, a special daughter who takes me to all my doctors and shopping and everywhere I need to go. She and Randy take me out to eat with them and invite me along always. I also am proud of my seven grandchildren and have an adorable great granddaughter. Ricky and Joanne separated during the time I lived in my Rolling Hills condo and he moved in with Lisa and Randy. Unfortunately, that wasn't working out. Then Lisa and Randy suggested I let him move into my condo at Rolling Hills and that we should buy a large house together. We bought in a new area in Davie called Ivanhoe and loved that house. We got along well, Lisa got pregnant while we were living there.

I was working in my office when Joan, the girl at the front desk came back to my office. She said she had to leave. She asked me to get another girl to take her place because she had to go to the hospital.

Her daughter was in labor. I said she must be mistaken. Her daughter's twins were not due until May. This was only January 22nd. Mary Ellen gave birth to two preemies weighing only a little over a pound each. Lisa, who was due to have her baby, delivered Zachary, her second son on the following day on January 23rd by C-Section. Lisa was in the room next to Mary Ellen, whose tiny babies were in a special preemie ICU nursery. Zachary was in the newborn nursery. We could see him through the window. He had red hair and was an adorable big baby. Someone looking at the babies said, "there's a linebacker for the Miami Dolphins". He was special too. Zach never liked Naples and after he graduated from high school he moved to Colorado. He seems to be very happy there. He is a free spirit. He has made many new friends and has a girlfriend. He calls us occasionally.

Although we loved our Ivanhoe house and had great neighbors, the Boyle family on one side and Mr. and Mrs. Thompson on the other, we needed something larger. They were developing a new section in Miramar called Silver Lakes with new large models at great pre-construction prices. We were lucky to sell our house in Ivanhoe and buy the new G.L. home in Miramar. I had my own quarters which were separate in a private area. What had been two average size bedrooms was made into one large suite for me and I had my own bath. Lisa and randy had the master bedroom and bath and the boys had their own rooms and bath. It was perfect.

CHAPTER **42**

ONE NIGHT I got up around 4 a.m. to go to the bathroom I got dizzy because I jumped up too fast and fell down on the carpeted floor. I was in terrible pain and unable to move. I started calling "help" but nobody heard me. It was a very large house and my area was private and so far away that Lisa thought a cat was meowing outside. Finally, around 8 a.m. they found me and called 911. The paramedics came but I was in too much pain to get up on the gurney. They put a contraption around me, half on one side and half on the other and scooped me up on the gurney to get me in the ambulance. They gave me pain medication immediately in the hospital and cut my nightclothes and underpants off with scissors. I had broken my femur off completely just under the hip-joint and it was crushed as well. Lisa called Jay, who was in Tampa. He cancelled all his patients and flew right over as soon as he heard. They had to find a special orthopedic surgeon to operate and repair all the damage.

He had to implant a long rod to replace the torn-up femur. It was a long surgery and a long painful recuperation process. Just before I went under I heard someone say I would never walk again. They didn't know stubborn me!

The morning after the surgery a psychiatrist came into my room. He started asking me questions. First, he asked my name and age. Then he asked who was president of the U.S., then he asked if I knew what month and year it was. It was my turn to ask him questions, so I asked him why he was asking me all these silly questions. He said it was because sometimes when a person has such a traumatic injury and lengthy complicated surgery, it affects their memory. As soon as they could move me, they transferred me to another hospital by ambulance where they had better facilities for care and rehab. The doctors Lisa worked for belonged to that hospital so they visited me every day when they made rounds. The nurses asked me if I was someone special because I had so many doctors come in to visit me. I was there for 30 days and in rehab for another 30 days. I named the physical rehab area (where I got therapy) the torture section. The therapist assigned to me was really thorough and tough. I asked her if she was a drill sergeant. She said she was! During the time I was there, she had to leave to do national guard duty, but came back after a weekend away. I was finally discharged after two months but was in a wheelchair and could not walk much, with a walker. I had to have a private nurse caregiver from 9 a.m. to 5:00 p.m. weekdays while Lisa was away at work. I had a beautiful, intelligent Haitian girl named Yoland. She called my injured leg the "aye aye aye" leg because every time anyone came near it that's what I hollered. I also had a home health nurse and physical therapist coming. By Christmas I was able to get around alone.

CHAPTER **43**

BETWEEN TAKING CARE of me and her job which was becoming very stressful, Lisa was ready to have a nervous breakdown. They had been having a house built in Naples which they intended to flip and sell. Instead they decided to move to Naples themselves. They sold our Miramar house and prepared to move. When Lisa told her boss, she figured out a way she could still work for him from home on the computer doing the billing and collections and drive across Alligator Alley to the Aventura office one or two days a week. She trained the girl who would take over her job as office manager and it has been working out well for her.

I moved with them but was unhappy. Randy's business was hit hard by the recession. He started over in Naples but it was a struggle getting going. I was not happy. I missed my friends and didn't know anybody. I drove to Pembroke Pines and rented a one bedroom apartment in century village and signed a four-year lease from March 2006 through March 2010. About 3 weeks after I moved into the condo Rick invited us all over for a home-cooked Mexican dinner. We all enjoyed it, but that night I started having very severe stomach pains. I was alone so I pushed my Lifeline button and the paramedics came and took me to the hospital. I had an intestinal blockage. I had surgery. When I was discharged, a nurse came daily to repack the incision. It took four months to heal. Finally, I started to feel better and was looking for something to do so I started volunteering for the Make-a-wish foundation.

It was interesting, stimulating and fun. The wishes that were granted to the terminally ill children were amazing and gratifying. Most of the people there were volunteers with only a small professional staff receiving a salary. Almost all of the money that came in from Fundraisers went directly for the children's wishes. Some kids wanted to go to Disney World, some wanted cruises, others wanted to go to the Florida Keys and swim with the dolphins, and many wanted to go shopping. Girls wanted new clothes and new bedroom furniture, while boys were into electronics and computers. Make-A-Wish is for real and not a scam like so many charities. I made a new friend and we went to the movies, out to eat, and to the shows and activities there.

CHAPTER **44**

DURING THE TIME I lived in century village some of our cousins from Detroit managed to find me. They were driving in Delray beach and saw Flip's office sign on the street in front of his office, went in and asked the secretary if they could see Mr. Friedland. They told Flip we had lost contact and they never gave up. They had been looking for me for ages. They had even placed an ad in the newspaper which I never saw. We have become very close to cousins Charna and Joel, after I moved to Naples we kept in touch. Lisa worked from home, but one salary was not enough. Randy had to keep driving across Alligator Alley everyday for work and because of the recession his customers were not paying. The housing situation was bad and their house was upside-down. They owed far more than it was worth. Their bills were piling up and the bank foreclosed on the house. They filed bankruptcy. They now had bad credit, but needed another house. I told them to look for a new house and I would buy it for them in my name. My lease was almost up on my rented apartment, I was starting to have some health problems. We decided I should move back to Naples and live with them, instead of paying monthly rent. I needed them and they wanted me back.

I paid some of the down payment, they paid the rest of the down payment and they would make the monthly mortgage payments thereafter. I gave a lot of my furniture to my grandson, (Flip's son) Alan, and his new bride, Nicole. Whatever they didn't want I gave to some needy Haitians and Good Will. I had my apartment cleaned. Randy came with a rented truck to get the rest of my belongings and move me to Naples. Randy was introducing himself to Naples condo management companies and getting acquainted with managers of their properties. They quickly learned that he did excellent work as a state-licensed pool contractor. He solved problems, was dependable and was right there when an emergency came up. When the managers changed jobs they obtained more pools and fountains for him to take over. He was getting so much work he needed to hire help and no longer had to drive across Alligator Alley. Thank goodness he's doing well and has more employees.

CHAPTER **45**

WHENEVER AUNT HANNAH went anywhere, people said "here comes Hannah with her children", even though she didn't have her children with her. That's because all she ever talked about was her children. They were her whole life. My sister, Lil, talks about her children all the time, too. Now it's my turn to talk about my children. Rick was my first born and very smart. He had a brilliant career as Regional Customs Counselor for the southeastern United States. Our next door neighbor in North Miami Beach worked for the secret service and told Rick about the opening for an attorney with U.S. Customs. He made an appointment for Rick to go for an interview with Dennis Snyder, the current regional counselor. As Rick was driving onto the highway the car in front of him stopped short and the car behind him hit him. The police came and helped him pull his front bumper away from his front tire. He was not charged with the accident and was given an accident report.

Of course, this made him late for the job interview. Dennis told his secretary he didn't want to see the applicant if he couldn't even be there for the interview on time. Rick showed up with his dirty hands holding the police report in his hands. When he told them what happened, Dennis agreed to see him and hired him. Rick had an amazing career with U.S. Customs, became regional counselor for the entire southeastern U.S. and handled cases which he was unable to talk about. He had to testify in congress and was involved in unbelievable legal situations. Recently a book was written by one of his peers about a customs case, entitled "Infiltrator". Rick was in charge of all the legal work and this was made into a movie. Of course all the names were changed in this true story. At Rick's retirement party, federal employees and attorneys attended from all over the country. Dennis told the story about hiring him although he was late.

Rick didn't do as well with personal life. He and his wife got divorced. She wanted children and he did not. He remarried the wrong woman. It would take several books to write how evil she was. Sadly, he was afflicted with Parkinson's disease and cancer and now is a very sick man. The only good thing that happened to him is his caregiver whom I call saint Elizabeth. Nobody could take care of him like she does. He lives with her family in Jacksonville. She takes him to the

Mayo Clinic for his appointments and takes excellent care of all his needs.

As I mentioned before, Flip became a C.P.A., he and Connie have three great kids. Alan (named after my Al) was born in January of 1984. He was a very good baby. He also went to FSU and is now a C.P.A. While in college he met his beautiful wife, Nicole, at FSU. Their wedding was an extravaganza on November 13, 2010. She was an only child and her parents went all out. My first great grandchild, Lily, a beautiful, extremely smart baby was born in January of 2014. Connie and Flip's second son, Michael, was born in June of 1985. He has always been fun. He went to college and has always had a good job. He is still taking some more college courses. He met Lexie in Tallahassee where she was going to college, too. On June 18, 2011, they were married at the Palm Beach zoo. It was a hot day but it was a very different, fun wedding. During the ceremony, the zoo animals were making noises. The ceremony had to start over several times because everyone was laughing hysterically at the noises. Michael recently changed jobs. He moved to Lake Mary and is now working with his cousin, Jared and is much happier. He and Lexie are a great couple. My only granddaughter, Stephanie, finally was born in February of 1988. You couldn't ask for a sweeter girl. She works with computers, which I can't do. Good things come in small packages and she is very petite. When the kids were all in school, Connie went back to teaching first grade at Spanish River school where she taught until she retired in June 2015. Flip is so lucky to have her. She's a wonderful person. During tax season, she works in Flip's CPA office, Flip became a "birder" and his hobby is taking pictures of birds. He gets up early to take the most amazing pictures. They are awesome and very real!!!

Jay went to school until he was 35 years old, between college, graduate school, medical school, internship, and residency. He specialized in male prostate cancer at Moffitt cancer center in Tampa, Florida, where he still did research, taught, and treated patients. He used the latest radiation methods like seed implants and the cyber-knife, Laura went to nursing school. They had my first grandson, Daniel, in Tallahassee in July of 1983 and Jared (their second son) in Gainesville in October of 1986. While he was working at Moffitt, Jay was offered a partnership in private practice in Delray beach, FL. He gave notice he was leaving Moffitt, they sold their Tampa house, rented a house in Delray beach, enrolled the boys in a private school and moved there. On the Saturday before he started working with the new doctors, Jay went to the new office and started to look through the files. He wanted to learn about their practice and familiarize himself with patients names. He felt something wasn't right and kept looking until he realized that they were fraudulently billing Medicare. When he confronted them, they didn't deny it. He said there was no way he wanted to be affiliated with dishonest doctors. They had signed a yearly lease on the rented house and paid a year's tuition at the boys private school and couldn't get their money refunded. They decided Laura and the kids would stay there for the year. Jay went back to Moffitt and stayed with friends until he could find a place to live and asked for his old job back. The hospital administrator said he was thankful that his prayers had been answered. He didn't want to lose Dr. Jay. They were going to take turns going back and forth between Tampa and Delray beach.

The boys were on soccer teams and had other activities on weekends. It ended up that Jay was making the trip most of the time after working a busy, tiring week at the hospital. When Laura had to go somewhere I would drive up and babysit the kids. The first thing I had to do when I arrived was go to the supermarket with Daniel and buy food. The refrigerator was always empty. I would buy the ingredients so I could make them their favorites like brisket and chicken soup. I drove to Delray beach from Davie to take Daniel for his driver's test in my car. After the year was up, Laura refused to go back to Tampa. She had made new friends and loved living at the beach. Jay was getting tired of traveling back and forth. This went on for quite a while. It finally ended in a nasty divorce. Eventually he found Valerie. She had been married before, had an autistic, needy son, and was divorced. She was Puerto Rican, pretty, but demanding and high maintenance. She did not like Jay's two sons. Flip, Rick and Lisa told him she was trouble and advised him not to marry her, but he did, anyway. Jay was very smart about everything except picking women. He married her in a garden type wedding at his riverfront Tampa home.

When Jay was in medical school he sat next to a girl named Debby Freeman who was also going to become a radiation oncologist. Her specialty was breast cancer. She was with an oncology group in Naples who needed a prostate specialist. She talked Jay into moving to Naples and joining the group. They had the Cyberknife and other modern radiation equipment to work with. They gave him a great secretary/nurse named Jody. He loved his new office and co-workers. Lisa lived in Naples and she helped him learn his way around. They exchanged recipes and told each other about good restaurants. They had great times together. He made new doctor friends. His practice thrived. His coworkers liked him. He saved the lives of most of the patients he treated. His reputation was world renowned. He rented his house in Tampa to a nice family. When he first came to Naples he rented an apartment. Then he found a beautiful house which he purchased. It was modern, large, and had a great pool and patio. It was in a wooded area and very private. He hosted parties serving the gourmet foods he cooked and the wines he loved.

His sons came to visit him. They promised to finish college. Daniel, the older son, graduated from the University of Central Florida and moved to southern California. He worked as a bartender while he got his masters' degree. He met future bride, Becky, a teacher and they were married on June 23, 2012. We went to their beautiful wedding in California. He got a good job, they bought a home in San Clemente near Becky's parents. They come to visit us on vacations.

The younger son, Jared, also graduated, became a talented graphic artist and was hired for a good position. When Jared was born, his grandma Kitty Conroy, said he looked like an Irish "Mick" so she nicknamed him Micky. He spends most holidays with the Friedland's. Close members of the family still call him Micky. He lives in Altamonte springs near Orlando now. But is very close to the Friedland's, especially his uncle Flip and family. He and Flip's middle son, Michael, are best friends and hang out together when they can.

CHAPTER **46**

UNFORTUNATELY, JAY DID not live to see his sons become fine young men. He would have been very proud of them. It started with a cough he could not get rid of. Then, he had pain in the kidney area which he thought might be kidney stones. Lisa urged him to have one of the doctors examine him and check him out. He had a kidney x-ray which revealed he had something there, further testing revealed a mass, which required a biopsy. The only one he confided in was Lisa. He asked her to promise not to tell anyone until he was sure what it was. Lisa was driving home from her office on alligator alley when he called and confirmed he had a malignant tumor. Lisa was driving and crying so hard she could not see. He said that since it was positive he would now tell the rest of the family. It was retroperitoneal liposarcoma, a rare cancer only four people out of a million are unlucky enough to get. He named it "the alien" which had invaded his body. It had to go. He prescribed his own course of treatment which consisted of surgery, radiation, and heavy duty doses of chemotherapy. Some of the treatment was at NCH hospital in Naples, where he served on the tumor board, and the rest at the Moffitt center where he had worked on cancer curing for so many years. He went into remission and we all sighed with relief. Then it returned with a vengeance. Nobody should have to suffer the way he did. Jody, his nurse and coworker was with him the entire time he was going through the excruciating treatment. She encouraged him and comforted him. She was his rock. She gave him hope and made him believe he would beat the alien and come back to work with her in the office. Jody still works for the same oncology practice with different doctors and we still see her.

Jay's wife, Valerie, left him in the hospital and took her illegitimate autistic son to Chicago to be evaluated. While she was away he took a turn for the worse. The hospital called Valerie on her cell phone and said somebody had to come to the hospital immediately. Valerie called Lisa late at night and told her that she had to go to the hospital right away to be with her brother. Lisa and Randy both jumped out of bed, got dressed and drove there as fast as they could. When they arrived, they found he had pulled out the I.V. and other tubes and had taken off his hospital gown. He was so out of it from morphine and other pain relieving strong narcotics he didn't know what he was doing. Lisa and Randy stayed all night taking turns watching him so he wouldn't pull everything out again. Jody came the next day and stayed with him. When she returned, Valerie gave everybody a hard time instead of thanking them. She screamed at Lisa and Randy and blamed them for what happened. She chased Jody out. Flipper and I lived on the east coast and she called us more than once and told us to rush to Naples if we wanted to see him before he passed away. When we got to the hospital she refused to let us go in his room Valerie wouldn't let anybody in to see him at all.

Towards the end, he asked where his mom was and said he wanted his mom. I was able to sit with him and hold his hand and told him it was ok. To go to heaven. His two sons had come and stayed in the room to be with him. They called their mother, Laura, Jay's ex-wife, who was now a hospice nurse. She drove from Satellite Beach, where she lived, to Naples to be with him at the end. She told him she always loved him and everything that happened between them was her fault. She did not stay for the funeral but was with him when he passed away peacefully on June 3rd, 2008 after fighting a valiant battle.

One morning before things got really terrible Rick and his second wife went to the hospital and invited the boys out for breakfast. They refused to go, saying they did not want to leave their dad alone because they did not trust Valerie. Ricks second wife called Valerie and told her what they said. Valerie called Daniel in the hospital room and told him to come there immediately and get his belongings and never come back to that house again. That only added to their heartache. The funeral was held in Naples on June 6th. I sat in the funeral parlor between Daniel and Jared and tears rolled silently down my face the whole time. There was a large picture of Jay and a video of his life playing. The funeral parlor was full. There were at least sixty doctors attending, some of whom gave eloquent speeches. His partner, Debby Freeman, could not praise him enough as a person and a doctor. After the funeral service, there was a celebration of his life at the beautiful Cypress Woods country club in Naples. I have to give Valerie credit for making that very nice. She probably did it to impress the doctors and other prestigious people there. I did not know for a long time what she did with his ashes. I finally heard that she threw them in the Hillsboro River behind his Tampa house, which he loved. But he lives on in my heart. I never saw or heard from Valerie after the funeral.

I have written about Lisa several times. I can never praise her or thank her enough for everything she does for me. Randy treats me more like a mother than a mother-in-law. His own mother, Ramona, says Lisa is one in a million. Nothing is perfect living together. There is a generation gap, and we have our differences. She is young and has hot flashes and I am old and cold with poor circulation, so it is hard to keep the house at the right temperature for everyone. Our likes and dislikes are different. We do a lot of compromising. It is hard for both a parent and adult children to live together. We don't think alike. They live in the modern technical computer world and I am still back in the old-fashioned days. In order for it to work, we need common sense and a good sense of humor. We love each other in our special relationship.

CHAPTER **47**

MY SISTER, LIL, said she's "better than some and worse than others". Right now, Lil is in her 90s and not well. I have a close relationship with Lil's seven children. I don't see them often but they know I love them. I am so lucky to have two sons, a special daughter, seven grandchildren and a great granddaughter. I also have two "almost sons" who call me "pro mom" and have adopted me. They are my late son Jay's best friend, Bob Singer, and Lisa and Randy's long-time friend, Warren. They're part of our family.

In October 2016, I woke up one day and was so dizzy with vertigo that I could hardly stand up. My phone rang and when I answered it I was unable to hear anything in my left ear. I called my primary care Dr. who referred me to an Otolaryngologist. He treated me with prednisone injections directly into my inner ear. He said I have Meniere's disease. It is an inner ear disorder caused by too much fluid in the inner ear, which causes hearing loss. Luckily, the treatment I was given restored some of the hearing and controlled most of the dizziness. It is a chronic condition. My Al would have said I am a "dizzy broad" (rest his soul). I am not allowed to use salt. Sodium is my enemy. I am only allowed limited caffeine like one cup of coffee daily, no alcohol or sodas. It is a nuisance trying to avoid sodium, but it could be worse. It's hard to go out to eat and choose the right thing if I don't want to have a recurrence, but it's not painful or fatal, so I am grateful. Except for arthritic joints which make walking difficult, and diet restrictions, I am ok. At least I have all my marbles. Jason gave me the name Mommo, because he could not say grandma. At his suggestion, I have written this and I titled it "Mommo's Story." This is written for my family and since I love every one of them. I am sure they will forgive me for any errors, omissions, punctuation or grammatical mistakes because I am far from being a professional author. But I am a "pro mom" and I did the best I could, without any professional training. I hope you all get some laughs and enjoy "Mommo's Story"!!!

CPSIA information can be obtained
at www.ICGtesting.com
Printed in the USA
LVOW07*1558210617
538884LV00011B/128/P

9 781478 789215